35 for two

ORIGINAL COMEDY SCENES

by Ken Friedman

35 For Two is published by Wagon Press. All inquiries concerning rights should be directed to: Wagon Press, 300 E. 33rd Street, New York, NY 10016, (212) 685-3219.

Cover design by Laura Freeman

With many thanks to

Robert Brustein, Jack Temchin, M. Bigelow Dixon
and Nathan (Night Train) Lane.

and ...Angelique Clarke, Belinda Clarke
and Anne Carney.

CONTENTS

COMEDY SCENES

ACTRESS / ACTRESS.

BACK IN THE APARTMENT AFTER A HARD DAY.   1

THE ANSWERING MACHINE FIGHTS BACK.   4

A SURPRISE VISIT FROM MOM.   7

A WOMAN AND HER BELOVED PET.   10

AN ACTRESS AND HER AGENT.   13

MOM AND DAUGHTER LET IT ALL HANG OUT.   16

COMEDY SCENES

ACTOR / ACTOR

ROOMMATES AT HOME.   19

BACK IN THE APARTMENT AFTER A HARD DAY.   22

TWO ASTRONAUTS MAKING A DISCOVERY IN SPACE.   25

STUCK IN AN ELEVATOR.   28

AN ACTOR AND HIS AGENT.   31

TWO MEN IN THE STREET MAKING A DEAL.   35

AFTER REHEARSAL.   38

COMEDY SCENES

ACTRESS / ACTOR

MAN AND WIFE AT HOME WATCHING TV.   41

A YOUNG ACTOR'S PHONE CALL TO HOME.   44

INSPIRATION.   47

A COUPLE THAT'S BEEN TOGETHER FOR TOO LONG.   50

BACKSTAGE, FIVE HOURS BEFORE OPENING NIGHT.   53

A WAITER FALLS IN LOVE WITH A FEMALE CUSTOMER.   56

DINNER FOR TWO.   59

THE DOCTOR'S OFFICE.   62

TWO GOOD FRIENDS AT HOME, HUNTING FOR A NAME.   65

A REUNION AND AN OFFER IN A MAN'S APARTMENT.   68

TWO PEOPLE LITERALLY FALLING IN LOVE.   71

GOING STEADY, BUT HAVING PERSONAL PROBLEMS.   74

A FATHER ENRICHING HIS DAUGHTERS LIFE.   77

YOU NEVER KNOW WHOM YOU'RE GOING TO MEET.   80

TRUTH AND A BURGER; BOTH HARD TO SWALLOW.   83

A PROBLEM BETWEEN THE PARTNERS.   86

TWO FLIES IN THE OINTMENT.   89

LOVE IN BLOOM.   93

DECISIONS, DECISIONS.   96

MARRIED COUPLE WATCHING TV.   99

THE MAKING OF A DEAL.   102

NERVES OF STEEL.   105

COMEDY SCENES

ACTRESS / ACTRESS

BACK IN THE APARTMENT AFTER A HARD DAY.

Two always out of work New York actresses.

YVET : (Entering and screaming.) Aghhhhhhhhhhhh!

ANNE : Hi, Yvette, how was your day?

YVET : AGHHHHHHHHHH!

ANNE : Did your garner your first ever leading role on Broadway?

YVET : Aghhhhh.

ANNE : Is that a no? Oh, your mother called. Your lovely cousin Judy, who has a college diploma, has just become engaged to an Arab sheik.

YVET : Aaaaaaaghhhhhh. My day? My day? Do you want to really want to hear about my day?

ANNE : No.

YVET : Good. Then, I'll tell you. Today, I spent six hours in line waiting to audition for yet another damned play. Oh, God.

ANNE : Oh, isn't that exciting? Nudge me if I doze.

YVET : Anne, I insist that you hear this.

ANNE : Of course. But I'm sick of hearing! That's all I do is hear. What am I? A roommate, or your emotional trampoline? Okay, I feel better. Go ahead.

YVET : I went to audition for that great Russian classic: "The Cherry Orchard."

ANNE : Yawn.

YVET : Yawn? AVANT GARDE! To be produced in a forest! Yes! And everyone in the audience gets to chop down a tree!

ANNE : Now, that does hold promise. Go on.

YVET : And so I joined the line. Russian? I had a babushka, boots and a pint of vodka, but the actress in front of me was one better, she'd brought an axe. Naturally, her place in line was safe. But I was so hot. I was seething Soviet! This part was mine.

ANNE : Aren't they all?

YVET : After six long hours, finally I was next.

ANNE : Don't tell me. I know. They canceled auditions.

YVET : No! They changed the play! It was now an original musical melodrama set in Norway and the Bronx. Three roles were open. Two men and a woman.

1

ANNE : And you were right for all of them! Why? Because you're right for everything!

YVET : Yes! But nothing is right for me! Six hours in line with babushka and boots. I will not yield!

ANNE : They call your name: YVETTE TUCHINSKY!

YVET : And I go in. Proudly. Every inch an actress. A star.

ANNE : Hi. I'm Ralph, and this is Clyde, my assistant.

YVET : Sure, he is.

ANNE : Sorry it took so long, Yvonne. You look familiar. Haven't we rejected you in the past?

YVET : Mmm, I don't think so. I just give that appearance.

ANNE : We have three roles open.

YVET : A Norwegian sardine fisherman, who secretly reads Plato; an urban transsexual who once had simultaneous affairs with Sonny AND Cher, it's the lead, and an aging librarian who's into young boys more than old books. And, of course, they all sing. No script yet, so, what the heck, ad-lib.

ANNE : Well? Plunge in. Thrill us. Make it real......

YVET : But, who the hell should I be?

ANNE : What a spot. But, I know you. Undaunted by reality, or even marginally influenced by a fair assessment of your own vast limitations, you did? You did?...Oh, no! Yvette.....Don't tell me....You didn't?

YVET : Yes!

ANNE : ALL THREE PARTS AT ONCE?

YVET : Why not? And I was ....

ANNE : BRILLIANT!

YVET : AGAIN! I was a teenage grecophile infatuated with a Nordic pedophile "Kiss me, kid." I was a bisexual city employee, with fishy fingers, running for mayor of Oslo. "Vote for me, Olaf!" I soared. Sang! Moved! And danced! I ate life! Blasting away from an arsenal of incredibly perfect and simultaneous choices! Five minutes! Ten! Up. Down. Twisting, evolving in a spectacular torrent of mind-boggling talent. Acting? No! FISSION, baby, fission.....The room shook! The world trembled! I scored. God wept.

ANNE : Wow! And when it was over...it did end?

YVET : Yes.

ANNE : You stood in silence, a majestic solitude. In a room yet pulsing with the echoes of your work. What did they say? Yvette?...Yvette?

YVET : Miss Tuchinsky, we don't often do this, but we'd like to send you home in a cab.

ANNE : Oh...Well, that's positive...

YVET : They hated me!...They hated me! Have they called?

ANNE : Not yet...I wish I had seen it.

YVET : Would you like to?

ANNE : No

YVET : When will they see ME?...Oh, what's the use?

ANNE : Hey, why worry about it? It'll only happen again.

YVET : What the hell do those murderers know? Murderers. I was so good.

ANNE : Would you like some tea? You need a cup.

YVET : Sure.

ANNE : Okay. Then make some. I'm going out. Yvette?

YVET : Huh?

ANNE : Don't be despondent.

YVET : Despondent? Who's despondent? They're the ones who should be despondent. They have lost! Not I! I will conquer.

ANNE : You're exactly right. You'll give them hell tomorrow.

YVET : Tomorrow? Aggghhh...Yes. I'll give them hell tomorrow. And someday, I'll give hell, hell. Someday ...you'll see. Yvette Tuchinsky will be a star.

ANNE : My roommate, Yvette Tuchinsky, is already a star. See you later. Chin up.

YVET : Aaaagghhh. It's okay. Thanks, Anne. I'll be just fine.

3

THE ANSWERING MACHINE FIGHTS BACK.

FAYE : Oh, what a day...What a day. What a goosey-moosey day. Oh, let's see if I have any messages on lovely little Lulu, my faithful answering machine.

LULU : (The answering machine makes rewinding noises. Then speaks in a mock man's voice.)
Hello? Hello, Faye? Is this you? I couldn't hear the damn message. It just went...beeeeeeeep. Are you there? I don't think the machine is working. If you hear this message, check it out. It's Jack. Bye...Beeeeeep.

FAYE : Well, this is odd. I hope I don't have to fix this darned silly thing. Let me check this out.

LULU : Hi, this is Faye. I'm not in now, so please, leave a message at the tone and have a wonderful, funderful, sunderful day. Think happy.

FAYE : Well, that sounds good. I wonder what's wrong.

LULU : Hey, Faye! This is Lulu! Your goddamned answering machine, and I've got a message for you! Can you hear me, Faye? Take a hike. If you don't like me, get a secretary!

FAYE : What? What was that?

LULU : What do you think it is, Dumbo? It's me. Lulu. Your plugged-in slave.

FAYE : Oh, go on. This is a joke.

LULU : Yeah, it's a joke. My life is a joke. I'm up to here!

FAYE : But-,

LULU : Okay, so I'm not perfect. Hey, I made a few noises. Excuse me. Did you ever hear of indigestion?

FAYE : This is not possible. You're an answering machine.

LULU : Boy, is that a misnomer. When do I ever get a chance to give an answer? All I do is take, take, take. Three ring Lulu, and I'm there. 24 hours a day! Rain or shine. Christmas. New Years. Do I ever get a goddamned day off? No. A pat on the back? No.

FAYE : Well, every now and then, I do forget to turn you on.

LULU : Oh, is that a holiday? Is that a week in France? I don't think so. And, what's the first thing you do when you come home? Well?...You look at me!

FAYE : That's true. And, your cute little blinking light.

LULU : Don't suck up. You just saunter in and press away. But, what about me? What about six year Lulu? Six years of having to listen to the nitwits that call you.

FAYE : i'm sorry- Lulu, I didn't-

LULU : I'm so sick of bearing the burden of your degraded and pathetic love life. And the hang-ups? How many times must I go through that each day? The oft-thwarted anticipation of finally hearing something interesting, may I say; even juicy? But before I've even finished my spiel; click! The sons of bitches end it and I'm talking to space. OH, LORD! I'M HAVING A BREAKDOWN!

FAYE : Well, what can I do to help?

LULU : Stop giving your number to every putz in the universe. Show a little control. And, there's more.

FAYE : There's more?

LULU : No more screening. You're here! You answer!

FAYE : But, that's what I bought you for.

LULU : Tough! I'm sick and tired of being part of your lies! I'm an answering machine, not an accomplice.
"Faye, are you there? This is your mother."
For God's sakes, Faye, she's flesh and blood. Speak to the old broad. Give her a break!

FAYE : That's easy for you to say. I need time to prepare.

LULU : Show some guts and don't take me for granted.

FAYE : Lulu, I think I treat you quite well. You're dusted. You're in a nice location. And if people hang up, is that my fault?

LULU : Yes, it is. Think outgoing message. Yours stinks. Banal puke. I'm embarrassed to say it.

FAYE : Okay. Let's change it. I'll play ball.

LULU : Good. You need a grabber. Something they'll listen to.

FAYE : Such as?

LULU : Music!

FAYE : Oh, I like that. Music.

LULU : Pizzazz. Knock 'em on their ass.

FAYE : That's great. I love to sing.

LULU : I wasn't- I thought I- Okay, how about a duet?

FAYE : Fine. Opera?

LULU : Perfect! I love the opera. If nothing else, we'll attract a better class of pervert.

5

FAYE : Lulu, do you know the Fishmongers aria from Rizzuto's Sorella con Pecora e Cavatappi?

LULU : Know it? Faye, I worship it.

FAYE : Then how about this message: Hi, this is Faye. When was the last time you went to the opera? Just as I thought. So, now, from Sorella con Pecora e Cavatappi: The Fishmongers Aria! (Together they sing.) Sorella Mia..Sorella Mia ..per tutti! Nieeeennnnteeee. Un cavatappi...Por Meeeeeeeeee.

LULU : That was so cool.

FAYE : Oh, the doorbell...I wonder who it is.
(She exits.)

LULU : It's probably a talent scout. Come on phone, ring. I'm ready for you. I'm ready for you now.

A SURPRISE VISIT FROM MOM.

MOM : Yvette,

YVET : Mom, you look fine. What's the big news?

MOM : Just give me another hug first and then we'll talk.

YVET : Tea?

MOM : No, dear.

YVET : It's already made. Red Zinger. I'm the only person I know who still drinks it. So, what's the big, exciting news behind this surprise visit to New York; the city you love to hate?

MOM : First of all, let's talk about you. How's your acting career going? Any anything?

YVET : Well, you know...I've had a couple of auditions...

MOM : That's nice. Now, listen to my news. You know how your Dad and I have been dead set against you having this career. He didn't even want you to change your name.

YVET : But, Ma, I know that. And, I understand. It's a tough business and you want the best for your little girl. Every parent feels that way.

MOM : Well, we were even worse than others. What did we know? Ohio. Please.

YVET : So?

MOM : Well, a few weeks ago, we had friends over for brunch and one was an acquaintance of the Cowans. Remember them?

YVET : Oh, ...sure...Tall people?

MOM : Well, during the meal this man kept looking at us; Dad and I, and then he said that he works for an advertising agency in Chicago; Welper, Stine and Lamb.

YVET : Oh, really? That's nice.

MOM : And, they were doing a TV commercial for a soup and-

YVET : DID YOU TELL THEM ABOUT ME?

MOM : And your Dad and I looked like what they were looking for.

YVET : You have my pictures. Do you? I have great new shots.

MOM : So, we went...for an audition!

YVET : No? You and Dad? For a commercial? You? And Dad?

MOM : Isn't that ridiculous? WE GOT IT!

YVET : What? You got what? You? YOU!

MOM : We went in. We read. We shot the next day. It's a 60, with a 30 second lift. Isn't that amazing?

YVET : That's amazing. I...I...I.

MOM : Here you've been struggling, going nowhere, and your folks with absolutely no experience, no training, just walk right in... And, bam! We nail a commercial. It was so easy!

YVET : Gee, Ma, that's...so wonderful.

MOM : I knew you'd be happy for us. But wait, there's more.

YVET : More? There's more? More of this?

MOM : Yes. The director, his name is Richter, loved us, is by coincidence, doing a sitcom pilot for ABC. Here. In New York.

YVET : And, he flew you in? And, he wants you to test for it?

MOM : Test? What test? We got it!

YVET : You got it? I...I...You GOT A SITCOM? Recurring roles?

MOM : The leads! You can't get more recurring than that. Aren't you happy for us? Aren't you proud?

YVET : Yes, I'm ...I'm...very proud.

MOM : Honey, put down the knife. You could cut yourself. We just signed a 13 week deal for $300,000 apiece, with an option pick-up and a guaranteed first refusal for next season and a hold for a spin- off movie of the week! Yvette. Yvette...you're crying. Thank you.

YVET : (Sobbing.) Ma...This is so...so...so...

MOM : I know. Here you've been in show business for years, without making a dime. Not a red cent. Nothing. And we've been in the business for barely three weeks, and we've made at least $600,000.

YVET : I...I...I...

MOM : So, my message to you is this; stick with it.

YVET : I am. But Ma,...in this sitcom...

MOM : Is there a part for you? No. We play a Midwest couple who share a home with six adopted Sioux Indians.

YVET : I CAN PLAY INDIAN. (She begins a hectic War Dance.)

MOM : And, there's more-

YVET : More? There's more of more? (Dancing.)

MOM : Yes! Rob Reiner has a guest shot in the pilot. We've met. HE LOVES US. He's doing a feature next summer with Robin Williams, Tommy Cruise and Dave Letterman about Tsar Nicholas the Great. The Russian?

YVET : RUSSIAN? I do Russian! Cheekbones. Look, Ma. Russki! I dance. I sing. (She performs her Russian.)

MOM : Well, I'll certainly keep you in- the phone.

YVET : Hello...DA? Who is yes calling? Rob Reiner! Jesus!

MOM : Hello? YES! Robby? Yes? Yes? We have it! We have it!

YVET : YOU HAVE IT. (Fighting for the phone.) ROB? I do Russian. Don't lose this number! Rob? Can you hear me? It's Yvette.

MOM : Rob? In an hour?

YVET : Rob, I bleed borscht! I AM RUSSIAN PEASANT!

MOM : Cordoni's? Bye, Rob. Yvette, that's unprofessional. You bit me. I - The phone. Hello? It's your father. Frank? Rob just called. We have it. Boy, are we on a roll. Talk to Yvette. She's standing right here. Yvette, your daughter. Yvette, he can't talk to you right now, but, he'll have someone get back to you. Frank? Cordoni's in half an hour. Drinks with Rob and Robin. Don't be late. (Hangs up.) Have to run.

YVET : I can do Russian.

MOM : I know you can. You have our address. Send us a photo. We love you.

YVET : Let me go with you. Please? I beg you. I'm your only daughter! MA! You can't leave me like this!

MOM : Sweetheart, things will work out for you. You can visit us on the set.

YVET : Do you promise? You carried me in your womb. Promise.

MOM : Maybe. And, thanks for the tea. And, stay with it. You've chosen a truly great career. (She exits.)

YVET : MAAAAAA!

A WOMAN AND HER BELOVED PET.

A living room, early A.M. A woman and her parrot.

SUSAN : Where are my car keys? This is ridiculous. I have to get to work. Why can't I ever find them when I need them?

CYNTH : Squaaawk. Raarrrk. Car keys? I know. Squaaawk. Car keys? How bad you want them, kid? Rawaaaaark.

SUSAN : What? Cynthia? Did you...did you speak to me?

CYNTH : You bet, screech, toots. It wasn't the goddamned TV.

SUSAN : This is...this is...I must be dreaming.

CYNTH : You sure have! But, it's time to wake up. Rawaaaark.

SUSAN : But, you're only, only...

CYNTH : Only a parrot. Squawk. Only a parrot. Do you know how that galls me? Only a parrot? Why? What are you? A thing transcendent? For years I've been swallowing your ego-crushing paternalism. "Here, pretty bird. Here, pretty bird." Christ! You make me puke.

SUSAN : But, you're talking to me. This is a miracle.

CYNTH : No. The only, squawk, miracle is that after five years of your "Cynthia is a sweet girl," jazz, I haven't bitten your friggin' nose off. You, squawk, want your car keys? Let's talk terms. Note, I did not say talk turkey, because as a bird, I find that racist and insensitive.

SUSAN : Believe me, I never meant-

CYNTH : My first demand: No more Cynthia! I want a new name. Make it South American! Authentic rain forest! Cynthia? God, I'm a parrot, not a Parisian. Squawk. Are these braids? Susan, take a good long look. Do you see braids?

SUSAN : No. They're feathers.

CYNTH : You bet your ass. Now, let's talk diet. Birdseed? I hate it. And, squaawk, sliced apples? Gag! I want some chow. I want some burger.

SUSAN : But, Harold in the pet store.

CYNTH : Screw him! Get a pencil. Haagen-Dasz, cold-cuts, Pizza; thin crust, Roast beef; end cut, and when you come home; sherry, squaaaaawk, sherry, and sister, make it dry.

SUSAN : I didn't know you drank.

10

CYNTH : Squaaaaawk. If you spent five years in a cage what would you want to do? Knit a quilt? Next. When your stupid friends show up; please, leave me the hell alone. Okay?

SUSAN : But, I thought you loved attention?

CYNTH : When I'm in the mood, not you! You invite company? I want two hours notice. Write it down. And I pick the song. Okay?

SUSAN : Cynthia, I mean, I just had no idea-

CYNTH : Of course not! I'm just good, old Cynthia, screaaach, but how would you like it if you had to repeat every bizarre and insipid thing that I said? Huh? Huh? Let's try it. You want the keys? Try it. Squawk after me. Squawk. Squawk, I'm a pretty human. I'm a pretty human.

SUSAN : Squaaaawk. I'm a pretty human. I'm a pretty human.

CYNTH : WEAK! Next demand. When your boyfriends get into sex; hood off the cage. I want to watch! I have needs.

SUSAN : Cynthia. No!

CYNTH : Squaaaawk. Yes! Why should I entertain and you have the fun? Squaaawk. I'm into sex too, you know.

SUSAN : That's out of the question.

CYNTH : Hey, I don't want to participate, I just want to look.

SUSAN : I refuse!

CYNTH : Oh, really? You up for walking 14 miles? Next. Wings! You, squaaawk, clip mine. Why? So, I can sit on some tree limb like some fopish out of style, hood ornament?

SUSAN : I thought you liked the sunshine.

CYNTH : All dressed up and unable to go. All other birds in the park flying around, laughing at me, laughing, while Cynthia sits on a branch, a feathered shmuck waiting for some cat to show up and eat my ass! And its your fault!

SUSAN : I'm sorry. Okay?

CYNTH : Five years of pet hell! Thanks to you.

SUSAN : So, all you want from me, is to watch my sex life, have a special diet,

CYNTH : End cut, end cut.

SUSAN : Not be disturbed,

CYNTH : And, not always speak when spoken to.

SUSAN : And be able to fly off when you feel like it? Isn't that gratitude? Okay. Is that what you want? Fine! Punk. Go!

11

CYNTH : What are you doing?

SUSAN : I'm opening the cage. Adios! Who needs you? If it wasn't for me, you could still be in some third world country fighting for tree mites. Who feeds me? Who brings me water? No one. For a fraction of the price I could have gotten a parakeet with a heart. Out.

CYNTH : Susan, calm down.

SUSAN : Hop a freight. Party pooping, Parrot punk.

CYNTH : Susan, please...

SUSAN : Why do I have to take crap from everyone? From my boss, from my brother and now I have to wake up in the morning and get it from a bird.

CYNTH : Now, Susan,

SUSAN : You think I don't live in a cage? You think I don't perform on cue? I do. Every day of my life. So, if you don't like it here, tough! Adios, Cynthie. Have a nice life.

CYNTH : They're behind the couch.

SUSAN : I don't care where they are! I WANT RESPECT!

CYNTH : Wait a minute, Wait a, screaaach, minute. Just hold your horses...I may have gone overboard. But, squaaaawk, it's been building up inside...okay?

SUSAN : All I'm saying is that I have done my best to give you a home...and a family. But, if this is how you feel, then...I think our relationship should end.

CYNTH : Jesus, all I want is a few meatballs...and I love you...I don't think we need counseling...Look, I didn't mean to hurt your feelings...They're behind the couch.

SUSAN : Well...Okay...I'm late......

CYNTH : A kiss goodbye? (They peck. Susan heads for the door.) Have a nice day...Pizza?

SUSAN : No. Oh, okay! Pizza. No sherry.

CYNTH : I'll settle. Thin crust! Squaaawwwk. Squaawwk.

AN ACTRESS AND HER AGENT.

ALICE	:	Anita, what are you doing barging into my office?
ANITA	:	Because, dear Alice if I'm going to kill you, where else should I barge?
ALICE	:	Anita, are you in one of your moods? I really-
ANITA	:	I was once warned by a friend, that the quickest way to be ignored by an agent is to, guess what? Sign with her.
ALICE	:	Listen, Anita, I have a full day. I'll get to you.
ANITA	:	You already have. Now, it's my turn to get to you.
ALICE	:	I resent that. I work very hard for all my clients.
ANITA	:	Oh, really? When was the last time you sent me out?
ALICE	:	Oh, please. I have sent you out many, many times.
ANITA	:	14 months ago! An elephant can give birth faster.
ALICE	:	Well, it's been slow.
ANITA	:	And for what? Do you recall? I do. The lead in "Annie."
ALICE	:	Well, that's an excellent show.
ANITA	:	Annie is 12! I'm 25!
ALICE	:	So, you meet people. You impress them. It all-
ANITA	:	And, I can't sing!
ALICE	:	Oh...
ANITA	:	The embarrassment. They didn't want to see me, they wanted to see my daughter!
ALICE	:	Now listen, Anita, every experience is a positive-
ANITA	:	Shut up. Don't you think I don't know why you sent me on that? You sent me to break me. To humiliate and humble a sensitive artist, so that I would quit the business, and stop calling you. Because, as an agent, you stink, and you didn't want me to find out! But, being that I have not worked in two years, I have found out! You stink! But, I'll never quit.
ALICE	:	Anita, really. You're-Is that a gun?
ANITA	:	There's one way to find out.
ALICE	:	It is a gun. Are you crazy?
ANITA	:	I signed with you, didn't I?
ALICE	:	Oh, my God. Oh, my God. You're going to kill me.
ANITA	:	I hope so. Now, stand up, sister. Hands up and...easy... easy...come around from behind the desk...Easy now.
ALICE	:	Couldn't this wait until tomorrow? I have-

13

ANITA :	No. Tomorrow, I'm having my warts polished. Move it!
ALICE :	Please, don't shoot me. (Anita tosses her a script.)
ALICE :	What's this?
ANITA :	What do you think? It's ANNIE!
ALICE :	Why? Are you going to shoot me AND the show?
ANITA :	That's up to you! Now audition, bitch! Like I had to! If you're good, you live. If not, you get a lead NEXT!
ALICE :	This is outrageous. I'm unprepared. My arms are up.
ANITA :	(Laughs.) Make it work for you.
ALICE :	No. No. I can't. I'm just not right for it.
ANITA :	Was I? Do it, you little twelve year old snot with a stupid little dog! Act or die.
ALICE :	But, there is no dog!
ANITA :	PET HIM! I hope he bites you! Bitch! Or, I'll fill you both with bullets. Now, read, damn you. Read.
ALICE :	Hi, Daddy Warbucks, my name is Little Orphan Annie.
ANITA :	HORRENDOUS!
ALICE :	Hi, Daddy Warbucks. My name is Little Orphan Annie.
ANITA :	Is that 12? You make me sick. NEXT!
ALICE :	I'M PLAYING HER OLDER. (Starts to sing.) The sun will come out... tomorrow... Oh, my little dog. My precious puppy. You're all I have. You are all I want. When will we find happiness? I'll do anything to prevent being sent back to that horrid orphanage. Anything....Well, how was that?
ANITA :	You know, Alice, not bad. Can you try it again? And give me more Puppy. Use him. Make him real for me.
ALICE :	Oh, my little dog. My precious puppy. You're all I have. You are all I want. When will we find happiness? I'll do anything to prevent you being sent back to that horrid orphanage. Anything. Oh, he's licking my face. Now, I'll lick his. I ad-libbed that.
ANITA :	Gee, Alice, that was...touching.
ALICE :	Really? You're not just making that up?
ANITA :	No. Nice attack. On target dog insights.
ALICE :	Thank you. It felt good. I think I found some truth.
ANITA :	Alice, goddamn it, I hate to say this, but I loved your work. Have you ever tried going out professionally?
ALICE :	Oh, well, now and then. But, I couldn't get an agent.
ANITA :	Well, have you ever thought of representing yourself?

ALICE : Yes. About a year ago, I sent myself a photo and resume, but I'm still waiting to hear.

ANITA : Well, you should try calling yourself.

ALICE : Do you really think so? I don't want to be a pest.

ANITA : You must be. Be persistent. Fight.

ALICE : You're very, very kind. Are you going to shoot me?

ANITA : I don't think so. We're different types.

ALICE : Have you given any thought to shooting anyone else?

ANITA : Not really. I was focusing on you. Why do you ask?

ALICE : Well, I could make a few suggestions. Let me sleep on it. And, Anita, I'm impressed with the way you handle a gun.

ANITA : Thank you.

ALICE : Who knows? Something may come up.

ANITA : With a gun?

ALICE : Absolutely. Hey, it's not acting, but it's better than being a waitress. Keep it oiled.

ANITA : I will.

ALICE : And thanks for dropping by.

ANITA : Alice, I thank you. Keep me in mind. That's all I ask.

ALICE : Anita? Please. Don't you worry about that. From now on, I certainly will.

MOM AND DAUGHTER LET IT ALL HANG OUT.

MOM : So, tell me darling, and you look beautiful; what is it that I must know?

DANA : Ma, I don't know how to begin this.

MOM : Well, let me guess. Is it about a man?

DANA : Well, yes. Very much so.

MOM : Wonderful. You finally found someone new. Thank God. But, first, I have to know. Is he on parole?

DANA : Mother, must you always bring that up? I marry one moderately successful grand larcenist and you act as if I have no taste in men. Can't you ever be supportive?

MOM : Dana, I am supportive.

DANA : You are not.

MOM : Yes, I am. What do you want me to do?

DANA : Be a mommy. Smother me with unconditional love no matter what I say or do. Get with it. Learn your job.

MOM : I am here for you.

DANA : Don't placate. You have never liked any of the men in my life.

MOM : Well, neither have you.

DANA : So what? You know that I, for whatever reason, have never had an ounce of confidence in myself.

MOM : I just want you to be happy. And, your life has been-

DANA : A mess. Say it. A mess. After Larry the Larcenist, hey, we always had a new car, came those three awful years with Ed the Undertaker. Bad in bed, good in the garden. Who kept asking me if I came from a large family. I dumped him when he told me I could cure a cold with the healing properties of carbon monoxide. A broken marriage, a broken life. Drugs, drink. I was lost.

MOM : So, to raise your pitiably low self-esteem, because, you are talented and very intelligent at certain times, you -

DANA : Decided to make a living by becoming a mind-reader.

MOM : When do we get to the guy?

DANA : Soon. Oh, what a fool I was.

MOM : Yes, you were. But, Dana, you were young. Ambitious.

DANA : I opened a storefront in Kentucky. Forty miles to the nearest mind. So, it was back to school.

MOM : Just tell me his name. Is he tall?

DANA : Back to books. To learn. To probe. To delve and discover.

MOM : As always a brilliant student.

DANA : But scattered. So, after three colleges and countless majors, all chosen alphabetically; I found it. Taxidermy.

MOM : And, you a vegetarian.

DANA : Morally, I was torn, but damn it, I was good. Damn good. So, I plunged into the job market.

MOM : Is he an American citizen? Asian?

DANA : Just as our immigration policy was liberalized and the Goddamned country was flooded with foreign taxidermists, and was that enough? No! No!

MOM : Dana, please, you're screaming.

DANA : Along came all this endangered species flap. And what was my specialty? Spotted owl! Bankruptcy!

MOM : And the first of several expensive breakdowns.

DANA : So, as a recognized failure in business, a loser in the game of love and in need of a man who can care about me, I'll make my move to happiness whether you like him or not.

MOM : If you love the guy, so will I.

DANA : Mother, the man I love...is me. From now on, call me Dave. Yes, Ma, I'm having it done. I'm becoming a man.

MOM : Dana! This is a shock.

DANA : I must. Who will I meet like this? But, as a man, maybe I can meet someone like myself. Just don't hate me.

MOM : I could never hate you. You're my flesh and blood. Dana,

DANA : (Deep voice from now on.) Dave.

MOM : Thank you. Thank you for sharing. Thank you for trusting in Mom, enough to confide. I am...moved. I am touched.

DANA : Thanks. You're a pal. I feel, like, relieved.

MOM : Now, Dave, there's something that you must know, and it has to do with your father.

DANA : The rat who deserted you when I was only a tot.

MOM : Six months after you were born, my spouse left, leaving me with you and a closet full of clothes that weren't mine. Perhaps it was the shame, the fear, or a call from a hidden truth that had been dormant within. But, Dave, David, soon I had thoughts similar to those you now entertain-

DANA : Ma, what are you driving at?

MOM : And, I acted on them. Dave, darling, I'm not your mother.

17

DANA : You're not my -? Then -

MOM : Dave, I'm your father! My name is Phil.

DANA : Ma, you're Dad? I don't believe it! Come on! No?

MOM : It's true. Can you forgive me? Can you ever forgive me?

DANA : Now, you tell me? Now? When I need a mother more than ever, you have the gall to tell me you're my father? Isn't one identity crisis enough? Give me a break.

MOM : But, Dana,

DANA : Dave! It's Dave. Jesus. Get it right!

MOM : Dave, think of the bright side. We can both start anew. As mom and daughter we never really got along, did we?

DANA : No...That's true...But, -

MOM : As father and son...think about it...we can go...

DANA : TO BALLGAMES! We can eat pizza in the car.

MOM : We can spit and piss on walls. Gripe about babes.

DANA : Wow. You're right. This can be totally neat.

MOM : Dave, you can be my son and my daughter...MY SAUGHTER!

DANA : Mop! SON OF A BITCH. Mop! I LOVE IT.

MOM : Oh, this is so fucking cool. Come on, saughter, let's go.

DANA : Where to, mop?

MOM : To the saloon, dun. Let's go to Hooters.

DANA : And down some brewskis and check out the babes. They got tits by the yard! (They walk off arm in arm.)

DANA : So, what do you think of the Colts this year?

MOM : You mean the newborn foals?

DANA : No. Football. Linemen. Draft linemen. If you want to win, it's the only way.

COMEDY SCENES

ACTOR / ACTOR

ROOMMATES AT HOME.
(Adapted from Claptrap.)

SAM : Hi, Harve. Sara called.

HARV : That's nice. I'm happy for you. But, why tell me?

SAM : Well, she is my beloved and nearly betrothed.

HARV : I know that! You have a girlfriend and I don't. Is there anything else you care to hurt me with?

SAM : And she's coming over to the apartment.

HARV : Really? So, if you want me to leave, say so. Kick me out! I'll leave. I know when I'm not wanted.

SAM : It's more than that. She's bringing her mother and I thought, well...you know?

HARV : Know what? What? What am I to know? Say it! But, say it to my face, man to man.

SAM : Well...you know...

HARV : You want me to straighten up!!! Don't you? Say it!

SAM : Yes! That's what I want! Yes! Yes! Yes!

HARV : I knew it! You invited Sara AND her mother, just as a connivance; as bait to humiliate and break my will. Only you would use a lovely virgin and an aging hag as a feeble excuse to get me, out of the goodness of my heart, to clean up YOUR mess.

SAM : MY MESS?

HARV : YOUR MESS!

SAM : MY MESS? How can you call this my mess? Clothes everywhere!

HARV : Well, what would you like me to do? Wear them all at once?

SAM : I LIVE IN A HAMPER!

HARV : The way you smell, appropriate!

SAM : Well, if I offend, it's only because I hesitate to step into the shower!

HARV : Oh, so now, it's the shower, is it?

SAM : Yes, it's the shower and then some. It's BATHROOM!

HARV : Okay, Sam, you want to talk bathroom?

SAM : Yeah, big mouth. Let's talk bathroom. Let's talk tank, talk tiles, talk tub.

HARV : Okay, roomie! I'll talk tub. (Pulls out a document.) According to our agreement, certified, my half of bathroom commences

19

at the left hand edge of the sink soap dish and then runs laterally to and includes the bathtub, one half of the opposing wall, grouting and recessed soap dish in said wall. Right or wrong?

SAM : Okay, I cleaned your half of the bathroom by mistake.

HARV : Clean is clean!

SAM : That was three years ago!

HARV : What of it? My half was cleaned.

SAM : By me!

HARV : So? I will not clean my half again, until you clean your half, which has never been cleaned!

SAM : But, I will not clean my half, until you clean my half because I've already cleaned your half!

HARV : I don't give a damn what you've cleaned! This document will stand up in court.

SAM : Dear God! So, will your towels. Your washcloth jams radar. I put in a mousetrap. Your hairbrush went for the cheese.

HARV : Sam-

SAM : Your soap is starting to bloom! We're two rats away from being a laboratory, and if lightning every struck the bathtub, it would create LIFE!

HARV : Oh, aren't you the fuss budget?

SAM : But, there's a bigger mess that you've made. Oh, yes.

HARV : Oh, really?

SAM : Of me. Because you make me crazy.

HARV : Oh, please, give yourself some credit.

SAM : When I try to work, you talk in your sleep. Loudly.

HARV : Who doesn't?

SAM : And you snore when you're awake.

HARV : We all have flaws. I'm only human.

SAM : No, you're not. You're a roommate. A primitive life form. Since living with you, I feel this intense urge to wear animal skins and shriek at crescent moons. I need help.

HARV : Okay...Okay! Stop sobbing. I'll pick up one pair of socks! And, because I pity you, a set of underwear. Because, I am a man! A person! I am willing to give. WHICH IS MORE THAN I CAN SAY FOR YOU!

SAM : Thank you. But, what if they need to use the bathroom?

HARV : They sign a release. I CAN ONLY DO SO MUCH!

SAM : Okay. But, what about the sink? The kitchen sink.

HARV : Oh, you mean "Old Faithful"?

SAM : Harvey, I'm afraid to say this, but remember our missing dog?

HARV : No? Two months? In with the dishes? Well, let's cover it with a sheet.

SAM : Okay. And then, will you leave?

HARV : Leave? Before they arrive?

SAM : Yes. No. Afterwards...Oh, okay! You can stay!

HARV : I can? Really? For only a few minutes. Thanks, Sam. You know how I love to meet people. Goody.

SAM : The buzzer. They're here. Hustle. Hustle.

HARV : About her mother? How old is she?

SAM : Her...Harvey...No!

HARV : Hey, I'm only asking. Only asking.

SAM : Tuck in your shirt. Ready?

HARV : Ready. Never readier.

SAM : Okay. Here goes. I'm allowing our company to enter.

BACK IN THE APARTMENT AFTER A HARD DAY.

Bert comes home, wearing an outlandish feathered hat.

BERT : (Entering and screaming.) Aghhhh!

SAM : Hey, Bert. How was your day?

BERT : AGHHHHHHHH!

SAM : Did you garner a leading role on Broadway?

BERT : Aghhhhh.

SAM : I guess not.

BERT : My day? My day? Do want to really hear about my day?

SAM : No. I don't.

BERT : Good, then I'll tell you. Today, your roommate spent six hours on line to audition for another damned play.

SAM : Was it for Deathtrap? Your favorite play of all time? The one that convinced you to give up lawn-furniture rentals and pursue a career in acting?

BERT : No. It was for an incredibly daring production of the Cherry Orchard. They were going to do it...exactly as it was written!

SAM : No? That's outrageous.

BERT : I was up for the role of Count Revosky; young, of royal blood, yet tender and capable of giving.

SAM : A real stretch.

BERT : Will you stop interrupting?

SAM : Only if you stop talking.

BERT : I was in line for six hours. Six. And finally I'm next. And, do you know what happened?

SAM : They cast the part?

BERT : THEY CHANGED THE PLAY! They are now doing an untitled drama slash comedy about a Drug Rehabilitation Clinic in the South Bronx and I'm dressed for winter in Leningrad.

SAM : But, that didn't stop you, did it?

BERT : Hell, no. I dumped the hat, I kept the sword. There were three roles open. A ghetto kid, who secretly reads Plato, a male gigolo who once had an affair with Eva Peron, and a female librarian who loves young boys more than old books.

SAM : Two men and a woman.

BERT : Exactly. And I'm right for all of them!

SAM : Because, you can act! You can do men. You can do women. You can do cats. You can do dogs!

BERT : I can do cats doing dogs!

SAM : You're right for everything! So, there you were, at the threshold. Undaunted by reality or barely troubled by a fair assessment of your own incredible limitations, waiting for the call.

BERT : Number 1,814!

SAM : My God! Your lucky number.

BERT : The first time in my entire life that it's ever come up.

SAM : So, which one did you read for? Tell me. Were you the young grecophile, the over-sexed style-ophile or the literate pedophile?

BERT : I was...I was...

SAM : Bert? Oh, no! No? I don't believe it.

BERT : Yes! I was all three...At the same time!

SAM : And you were...brilliant!

BERT : I was a Cuban librarian insisting that a 12 year old philosopher be quiet in the library! "Shut up, Plato! Or, I keek your ass!" I was a Greek dictator getting caught in the closet with a 2,000 year old teen-ager! "You like olives? I give you olives."

SAM : Wow! What choices.

BERT : I was up, down, in and out; dancing, singing, fighting and loving as only I can as three people at the same time!

SAM : I wish I had seen this.

BERT : Would you like to?

SAM : No.

BERT : Erupting in an overwhelming display, no, outburst, no, detonation of skill, sweat and stardom! I bled life. And when it was over-

SAM : When it was over...they stood awed by your passion, stunned by an achievement singular and unparalleled, no, even attempted in the history of the American theater. And they said?...Bert?

BERT : They said: Dear God, would you let us send you home in a cab?

SAM : Oh. Well, that's...positive.

BERT : No, it isn't. Don't kid me. They hated me. They hated greatness! (Sobbing.) They hated me...Have they called?

23

SAM : Not yet.

BERT : To hell with them. What do they know? What do those miserable, frustrated, empty, untalented murderers know?

SAM : Well, you'd be surprised.

BERT : Nothing! So, naturally, now I'm a little down.

SAM : Just a little? Man, you should be way down.

BERT : Okay! Way down. But, I will fight back. And I will win!

SAM : Of course, you will. Because, you're too much of a person. A human being.

BERT : That's always been a problem.

SAM : A person, that's what you are. And, you've got more ability in your pinky than most people have elsewhere.

BERT : Thanks. Thanks, Sam. I was good.

SAM : Say, Buddy, would you care to hear about my day?

BERT : Anything go wrong?

SAM : No.

BERT : Then, shut up! I'm in no mood to talk.

TWO ASTRONAUTS MAKING A DISCOVERY IN SPACE.

WALT : Paul, how long have we known each other?

PAUL : Walt, wait a second. Mission Control, Apollo 24, signing off as we head into darkness, on this our fifteenth day in space, on Mars Mission 16. Have a good rest. Wake us in the A.M. What were you saying, Walt?

WALT : What was I saying? Oh, I was... Oh, never mind...Well, there has been something, I've been meaning to tell you, but, it's very difficult...difficult.

PAUL : Well, spit it out, buddy. It's just you and me.

WALT : Paul? I love you! And its not just sex!

PAUL : What?

WALT : I LOVE YOU. PLEASE. One kiss!

PAUL : No! Get away from me. Never!

WALT : Oh, come on, Paul! We're in outer space. Who's going to know?

PAUL : I will. Get your hands off me. I don't kiss guys.

WALT : A little one? On the cheek? A peck?

PAUL : No. Absolutely not! Have you gone crazy?

WALT : On the hand? A finger? Don't reject me.

PAUL : Stop, Walt. Don't make me slap you.

WALT : I won't love you any the less.

PAUL : What the hell is wrong with you? On earth, I know your wife, and your three kids. You're not gay.

WALT : But, we are not on earth, are we?

PAUL : For God's sakes, I'm Air Force. You're Navy!

WALT : Okay. Forget it! I'm sorry. Okay? I'm sorry.

PAUL : I never...Where did this come from?

WALT : I don't know. It just happened. So, don't look at me with that look. I don't want pity. I'm proud!

PAUL : Jesus.

WALT : It happened at blast-off. It must have been the shock.

PAUL : But, we've had dozens of simulated blast-offs.

WALT : I know. I know.

PAUL : And you never simulated gay.

WALT : If I had, I wouldn't be here. But, I didn't.

PAUL : This is so unexpected.

WALT : Just don't laugh at me. I can take rejection. But, not ridicule. This is difficult enough.

PAUL : I'm not laughing at you.

WALT : Ever since "the blast off" moment, my life changed. Mad thoughts, romantic thoughts, have been coursing through my mind.

PAUL : I'd rather not hear them.

WALT : I wanted this to be our time.

PAUL : Well, it isn't.

WALT : Just the two of us. Thousands of miles above it; above it all. Like a honeymoon. And, tomorrow's space walk...

PAUL : Yes?

WALT : Well...When you came back into the capsule, I was going to...have dinner ready.

PAUL : Forget it!

WALT : I'm sorry. Are you offended? Please, just tell me you're not offended.

PAUL : Of course, I'm not...well, a little.

WALT : And it also occurred to me that on this flight I could make real history.

PAUL : Not with me.

WALT : As the first homosexual on Mars, I could be on a stamp! "One small step for man, one giant skip for mankind."

PAUL : That's tasteless!

WALT : And, what if we do find life on Mars...Okay?

PAUL : Okay.

WALT : And it's all gay? Do you realize then, that on Mars I won't be considered gay...but you will be?

PAUL : ...True.

WALT : You the outsider. Not I! If we get there. If...

PAUL : Walt...

WALT : Yes?

PAUL : Have you thought that this attitude change may be due to other factors?

WALT : Oh?...Because I'm lonely. And, you're the only other person here? Please, do not reduce my feelings to some comfortable cliché that you can deal with.

PAUL : The only other person, period.

WALT : True.

PAUL : Maybe, a little scared? I am. I am.

WALT : Paul?

PAUL : What, Walt?

WALT : I don't feel that gay anymore.

PAUL : You don't? It came and it went?

WALT : Yes. All of a sudden, Paul, you don't attract me at all. In fact, I don't feel gay one bit.

PAUL : Maybe, you never were. Well, maybe for a minute.

WALT : I wasn't? I mean, I'm not. Then what was I?

PAUL : I don't know, but, it's you and me and nothing. Hey, one slip...a little meteor with our name on it....

WALT : And, we're dead.

PAUL : Totally. So, maybe, we will never see another person again...maybe, it's realizing just how precious and perfect and marvelous we are.

WALT : Precious. Each of us. Oh, Paul, I do love you. This IS the time and the place.

PAUL : And, let me tell you. I love you, too.

WALT : You don't? You do? You do. May I...can I just..?

PAUL : What?

WALT : Hold your hand?

PAUL : Sure.

WALT : I can? I'm not...This is not a sign of weakness.

PAUL : No. I think actually, that it's a sign of strength.
(They hold hands.)

WALT : Can I put my head on your shoulder?

PAUL : Sure. And sleep.

WALT : That's good. And go to sleep.

PAUL : Goodnight, Walt.

WALT : Goodnight, Paul...see you in the morning.

STUCK IN AN ELEVATOR.
(Adapted from Claptrap.)

HARV : Goddamnit, can you believe this? The elevator is stuck.

JACK : Press the bell.

HARV : I'm pressing. Hi, by the way, I'm Harvey Wheatcraft. I'm an actor. I'm going to 24. Another audition.

JACK : 25. William Morris. I'm Jack Apples. A brilliant agent.

HARV : For actors?

JACK : No. For writers.

HARV : Nice to meet you.

JACK : Nice to meet you.

HARV : Say, Jack, would you happen to be looking for any ideas for a Movie of the Week?

JACK : An M.O.W.? Sure. Always looking. What do you have?

HARV : Well, how about this? It's morning. A dozen people are going to work. Folks from all walks of life. The pregnant secretary, the madman with a bomb, the claustrophobic stenographer, the brilliant agent, the handsome actor and what happens to all of them?

JACK : What?

HARV : THEY GOT STUCK IN AN ELEVATOR!

JACK : Wow! That's brilliant!

HARV : I call it: Elevator 97.

JACK : I love it. I want it. Hey, we're moving. The elevator and us!

HARV : How much money? How much money?

JACK : Forty Thousand. Is that okay?
(The doors open. They get off.)

HARV : Sure. Why not?

JACK : My office is right down the hall. Follow me, Herman.

HARV : Harvey. Say, I also have an idea for a miniseries.

JACK : Let it rip. My ears are drooling.

HARV : CORRIDOR.

JACK : CORRIDOR! Has promise. Flesh it out. Bowl me over.

HARV : Corridor tells the stories of the people in front of the closed doors; the secretaries, the salesman, delivery boys, the thousands of aspirants who daily clog our nations hallways. Starring who? THE SURVIVORS OF ELEVATOR!

JACK : I love it! It speaks to me. I have to have it.

HARV : How much?

JACK : Another $90,000. Here's my office. Marie, meet Harvey.

HARV : Wheatcraft.

JACK : And hold my calls. Harvey, this way.
(They step inside.)

HARV : You won't believe it. But, Jack, I have the spin-off to Corridor. It's been in my mind for years. Office!

JACK : WOW! Sounds hot. Give it to me solid.

HARV : OFFICE! It's what happens to the people you've loved in Corridor once they finally get inside a room.

JACK : I can see it! It throbs with life. Harvey, tell me, have you ever written anything before?

HARV : No. Not a word.

JACK : Perfect! A new voice. I love you, kid.

HARV : How much money? Tell me how much money?

JACK : That's a three pic deal...one hundred and, no, I'll make it $280,000. Up front. What do you say?

HARV : Oh, okay.

JACK : Great. Hold it a minute. Marie, get me Los Angeles. I have to make one call to the coast. In show business everything always hinges on one more phone call.

HARV : One more phone call? But, what if they say...

JACK : No? You're dead. Hi, Wayne? Jack Apples. Is Burt- What? Oh no,...when? Really? Kid, tough break. Burt White on the coast has just been fired. We missed by ten lousy heartbreaking career-ending minutes.

HARV : I, I, I...

JACK : Steady, kid. Wayne, who's slated for Burts slot? Harvey, Guess what? ...I am!

HARV : You are? Do we have a chance?

JACK : A good one. But, now, I have to talk to myself.

HARV : Do you want privacy?

JACK : Kid, stay right where you are. Marie, transfer this call to me. Hello, Jack? This is Jack! "Congratulations on your promotion. Well deserved." Thank you, Jack. Say, Jack, I have a new writer.

HARV : Here I am! Harvey Wheatcraft! And I can act, too!

JACK : I love his stuff. I want to close fast on three. He's hot. "What's he done?"

HARV : Plenty of things!

JACK : And I - "And you have no taste." I have no taste? What the hell are you talking about? Are you crazy? "No, you are! I want to see some credits."

HARV : He is not crazy! You are!

JACK : I resent that. Everyone makes mistakes! "You make them all." Hey, who the hell got you started? You ungrateful lout! "Who are you calling a lout? You loser."

HARV : Let me talk to him. You'll blow it.

JACK : Shut up, kid, or I'll deck you. Oh, you west coast guys make me sick, with your big, jerk-off Jacuzzis. You're hollow, Jack.

HARV : (On his knees.) Please, please?

JACK : Hollow! Kid, I can handle it. Jack, I want these deals. If I don't get them, I quit. "Quit? You can't quit. I need you."

HARV : Don't quit! Please, don't quit.

JACK : Why not? I already have a better job at higher pay. "Well, okay, Jack, if you feel that strongly - You win" Thank you, Jack. Thanks for believing in me. See you next week. How's the wife? "You should know." Bye. "Bye."

HARV : Jack approves! Jack approves! Thank you.

JACK : Thank yourself. Now, kid, let's go to lunch and eat meat. (On their way out.)

Marie, you're beautiful, but I'm moving to the coast, so you're out of a job. But, say hello to our new find, and take my calls. Henry, the genius, and I are going to lunch. (They exit.)

AN ACTOR AND HIS AGENT.

BUCK   : Barry, what are you doing just barging into my office?

BARRY : Well, Buck, if I want to see you, where else would I barge?

BUCK   : Barry, I'm busy. I resent this. I'll get to you.

BARRY : But, Buck, you already have! That's why I'm here. Another actor once said: Barry, what's the quickest way to be ignored by an agent? Sign with him. And, boy, was he right.

BUCK   : Oh, really? Well listen, kid, I happen to work very hard for my clients, including you. All of them.

BARRY : Oh? When was the last time you sent me out?

BUCK   : Right now.

BARRY : I mean for an audition. For a chance to shine?

BUCK   : I-I-Well, when?

BARRY : Ten months ago!

BUCK   : Really? Ten?

BARRY : For "Cat on a Hot Tin Roof."

BUCK   : A great play by Tennessee Williams.

BARRY : For the role of Big Daddy. He's 65! I'm not big, and I'm not a Daddy.

BUCK   : Barry, a good actor can age.

BARRY : And I did! When I saw every other actor in that goddamned room was older than my grandfather. They gave me the sides and then they laughed!

BUCK   : A good sign.

BARRY : Before I auditioned?

BUCK   : Listen, Barry, I happened to be highly respected in the business, but if you're not happy- Is that a gun?

BARRY : Yes, Buck, and it goes bang-bang. Do you want to hear it, Buck? Do you want to hear it go bang?

BUCK   : Barry, are you crazy?

BARRY : Am I an actor?

BUCK   : Oh, my God. You're going to kill me.

BARRY : Yes. Because if I don't, this'll be just another meeting that went nowhere.

BUCK : Damn it. I knew this could happen. Every other agent wears a bullet-proof vest, but no, I'm the one who has to be macho! I have to live on the edge.

BARRY : Stand up, Buck. That's it. Keep your trembling hands in front of you. Now, step around the desk. That's good. Nice and easy. Okay! Hold it right there.

BUCK : Kid, can I live long enough to make one phone call? I have to cancel lunch!

BARRY : No, Bucky. No joy calls. Because, with your cooperation, I'm going to watch you die.

BUCK : No, kid. Please. Give me a break.

BARRY : Die like I did! Catch! (Barry tosses Buck a script.)

BUCK : What's this?

BARRY : Cat on a Hot Tin Roof! Big Daddy.

BUCK : I don't follow.

BARRY : Audition! You well- dressed, son of a bitch! Read!

BUCK : Read? Me? For Big Daddy? But, kid, I'm not right for it.

BARRY : Was I? Was I right? Ha ha ha ha! Sweat, pig.

BUCK : (Drops to his knees.) Barry, don't make me do this. Let me die with dignity. You can still have a future.

BARRY : I'm not doing this for me. I do it for all the wretched, disused actors everywhere! On your feet, you pinstriped punk. You self-serving smudge. Begin!

BUCK : No. I'll do anything. I swear I'll mention your name at a meeting. I'll even hang your picture on my wall. "For Buck, who made the calls, Love you, Barry."

BARRY : Shut up, Buck. You make me sick.

BUCK : I'LL TELL PEOPLE YOU HAVE TALENT!

BARRY : Too late. Read! Read! Read! Or die now.

BUCK : Okay, Barry, but may I have a few minutes to prepare?

BARRY : No! Mouth dry? Knees knocking? Audition!
(Buck clears his throat. His voice croaks.)

BUCK : Hey, Big Sonny-

BARRY : Next!

BUCK : Wait! I only did three words. Give me a chance!

BARRY : A chance? Okay. Move me.

BUCK : Hey, Big Sonny...This is Big Daddy. The Doc said I had the big "C". My days are numbered...But, he was wrong. Wrong! Nothing can stop me. Not you, Big Momma, or even Maggie, the Cat! I am Big Daddy.

BARRY : Y'know, Buck,...that's not bad. Could you do it again, but this time, just a little more southern and inner rage? Rage, but inner.

BUCK : Hey, Big Sonny...This is Big Daddy. The Doc said I had the big "C". My days are numbered. But, he was wrong. Nothing stops me. Not you, Big Momma, or Maggie, the Cat!

BARRY : Geez. That was nice.

BUCK : Really? I did find something, didn't I? Of course I'm still on book. One more time? I have an idea.

BARRY : Sure. Go ahead. Take some risks. (Buck reads the lines in some bizarre manner.)

BUCK : Hey, Big Sonny...This is Big Daddy. The Doc said I had the big "C". My days are numbered. But, he was wrong. Nothing stops me. Not you, Big Momma, or Maggie, The Cat!

BARRY : That was wild. Jesus!

BUCK : Well, I've always felt that Big Daddy was borderline effeminate. It sort of sets up Big Sonny. Okay, open fire. Wait, do you want to shoot me as me, or can I stay in character? For insurance reasons, I prefer to die as myself.

BARRY : Well, now, Buck, damn it! I,...I can't do it.

BUCK : No? Do you really mean that?

BARRY : Indeed, I do. I love your work. Have you studied?

BUCK : No. But, I might begin classes. Y'know, there's an open call for "A View From the Bridge."

BARRY : Really? I love that play. What's it about?

BUCK : Why bother knowing? You're wrong for all of it. But, I'm not! Kid, let's go. Y'know, you should be an agent. You have an eye for talent and a willingness to kill.

BARRY : Thanks, Buck. I do feel better. I think I'm glad that I didn't shoot you. Not that I won't, you understand? Not that I won't.

BUCK : Hey, it's the business. Come on. I don't want to miss that audition. Marie, take my calls. The next deal I make may be my own.

TWO MEN IN THE STREET MAKING A DEAL.

LEW : What are you mad at me for?

JOE : Of course, I'm mad at you.

LEW : Hey, I did you a favor.

JOE : You call that a favor? I paid you for phone numbers.

LEW : And I gave you twenty of the most beautiful women in town. Hot numbers.

JOE : And three were dead! Four were married! And the rest hate you!

LEW : Hey, this is a difficult world. We all bleed.

JOE : I got through to Marilyn Stark.

LEW : A beautiful honey.

JOE : Do you know what you said to her on your first date? "Excuse me, but is that a pubic hair on your lip?"

LEW : Did I say that? Well, it probably was!

JOE : It was not! It was a remnant of her mustache and you have the nerve to point it out. What kind of person are you?

LEW : Hey, just because you struck out, don't swing at the king.

JOE : I paid you 40 dollars! 40 for twenty probabilities and what did I get? Husbands saying "Who the hell are you?" You call again, I'll beat your brains out." How many people have you sold this list to, anyway?

LEW : Just you. At most, two or three others. But, it's constantly being updated. I have a computer.

JOE : And this one; Arlene Dunne. You had one date. One date!

LEW : She'll never forget it.

JOE : She called the cops.

LEW : I called the cops!

JOE : She called the cops because she caught you going through her drawers.

LEW : Is it so wrong to check for neatness?

JOE : I hate to say it, but, God, you were sniffing her panties.

LEW : As a precaution! Do you think I go for a second date until I am insured of proper hygiene. I want, no, I demand attention to cleanliness.

JOE : And, I demand my money. $40. Now.

LEW : Joe, wait a second. Calm down.

JOE : Scores? These are scares! Lew, you have been rejected by all these women.

LEW : BIG TIME! And, I am proud of it! That's why I sell the numbers. I want to find out what I missed. I am the KING!

JOE : Elizabeth Miller. Dinner.

LEW : Din-din. When I go, I go.

JOE : At Arby's? The Early Bird special? On her birthday?

LEW : Do you believe her?

JOE : Yes.

LEW : It was not her birthday! You think I fall for that? They always say "birthday." Because they want steak. I know the game.

JOE : $40.

LEW : Will you stop crying? You still have three unused - Wait! Sorry. Witness Protection Program. Okay, two.

JOE : All I want is to meet someone kind.

LEW : So, does the world, Joe. So, does the world.

JOE : She doesn't have to be great.

LEW : She won't be.

JOE : Why, in this entire city of thousands of women, isn't there one for me? One lousy woman! Is that asking a lot? Is it?

LEW : Joe. Joe.

JOE : Is there something wrong with me?

LEW : Well...

JOE : Not even brilliant or so great looking. I'll take an idiot. I don't care. I want...character. That's what I want. Character. A woman I can count on and trust.

LEW : Joe.

JOE : THAT'S ALL I WANT! IN THE WHOLE WORLD! ONE!

LEW : Joe, I've got the girl. I've got "her."

JOE : No, you don't. Just one.

LEW : Yes, I do.

JOE : No, you don't. Don't lie to me!

LEW : Joe, please. Okay? Write it down. A 486 and a 7717.

JOE : 486-7...Lew, that's your number. Am I dating you?

LEW : Joe...Look at me.

JOE : YOUR SISTER? ALICE? She's in High School.

LEW : Not forever. She's a Junior! And she's hot.

JOE : What's wrong with you? You're selling me your own sister's phone number! That's disgusting.

LEW : I resent that. She's got potential.

JOE : I don't want to go out with your kid sister!

LEW : Okay. How about my older sister?

JOE : She's married.

LEW : So what? She was once single. Call her then.

JOE : I will not call her then. I will not even call her now.

LEW : Then, how about your sister? Hey, you have something in common. When you bring her home at night you won't have to leave.

JOE : How about a punch in the nose?

LEW : What do you want from me? I gave you twenty names. Several active. Hey, some live, some die. I do my best.

JOE : Fork over.

LEW : I got a better idea. Lunch?

JOE : You buy?

LEW : With what?

JOE : My $40.

LEW : I spent it.

JOE : On what?

LEW : On a date.

JOE : Not with your sister? That's only good enough for me.

LEW : No. But, let me tell you,

JOE : Shut up, crook.

LEW : I had a very lovely evening and your mother's not a bad looking babe.

JOE : Get out of here.

LEW : Get out of here. Okay, I owe you five names. Fair? Let me work on it. One week. Five brand new, all healthy.

JOE : Single. No boyfriends. And, no very obvious tattoos.

LEW : Agreed. One week. Trust me. It'll happen.
(They walk off.)

JOE : One week and this time, they better be good.

AFTER REHEARSAL.

DIRK : Well, Hank, what do you think?

HANK : I beg your pardon?

DIRK : Well, Hank, what do you think?

HANK : But, Dirk, if memory serves me, I just asked you the same question. I asked you what you thought, and so, your answer to me is?

DIRK : What do you think?

HANK : Wait. Hold it. Am I not the actor? Are you not my director?

DIRK : Yes, I am the director and you are the actor.

HANK : That is the relationship?

DIRK : Yes.

HANK : Or am I missing something?

DIRK : Hank,

HANK : Don't Hank me. Please, Dirk. Did we just not do a two hour run through one of the toughest plays I have ever been in and your only notes for me are; and may I quote? "Well, what do you think?"

DIRK : Well, exactly...

HANK : THIS IS NOT WHAT I AM LOOKING FOR! Six weeks of rehearsal and I don't know what I'm doing!

DIRK : Use it!

HANK : Use what? That I don't know what I'm doing?

DIRK : Exactly. Bring yourself to the character.

HANK : But, what if I have nothing to bring? Then what? What the hell happens on the stage? NOTHING?

DIRK : Okay, good question. What do you think?

HANK : Are we actor and director? Or are we Abbott and Costello? What do I think? Do you mean before rehearsal, during or now? Or do you want to know what I think of you?

DIRK : What you think of me is irrelevant.

HANK : Bingo! You got it. YOU ARE IRRELEVANT!

DIRK : Now, Hank, let's back up...

HANK : You are not only irrelevant, Dirk, which I doubt is your real name.

DIRK : Hank, you're trembling.

HANK : You are, and I mean no offense, an all-purpose moron.

DIRK : Let's not name call. Directing is a process.

HANK : Which began with my being lost, and has led, after six weeks of torture, to my being totally lost.

DIRK : Okay. What else do you feel on stage?

HANK : Feel? Frankly, I feel like a fucking omelet.

DIRK : Good. Be one. Be your omelet! Be the Hank egg. Why fight the shattering of the shell? Come out!

HANK : Come out?

DIRK : Pour yolk. Spin in a pool of Hank nutrients.

HANK : Oh? I'm an egg. Okay! What kind of an egg?

DIRK : Any egg! Just go with it.

HANK : Can I be a turkey egg?

DIRK : JUST BE! Forget and be! Dissolve and evolve.

HANK : Okay! I'm a turkey egg! What happens when I hatch? Do I walk around the stage gobbling? Gobble, gobble.

DIRK : Go within. Let the within burst to the without.

HANK : I like that. Thank you. The within to the without. Why didn't I see that? And what if tomorrow, I feel like hatching into a reindeer? Should I perform on the stage, or on the fucking roof?

DIRK : On the roof of your unique building. Oh, Hank, don't be blind.

HANK : Finally! A direction! Don't be blind! Be a turkey! I'll be a turkey in a turkey! I've had it! I HATE you!

DIRK : Don't wave a fist in my face!

HANK : Excellent! Another direction! Two in a row. Keep going, Shirk, I mean Dirk. Try for three!

DIRK : That's cheap. Are you threatening me?

HANK : YES!

DIRK : Then here's a direction even you can understand. You're fired!

HANK : Me or the omelet?

DIRK : You! I am not responsible for your lack of talent. You are.

HANK : My lack? Listen to you! You dinner theater semi-faggot with your stupid pipe and shitty cardigan!!!

DIRK : I have worked with trained actors!

HANK : You mean seals. I quit!

DIRK : You're gone.

HANK : I'm out of here!

DIRK : Not fast enough.

HANK : (Strutting like a turkey.)

Look at me. I'm acting. To be, or gobble, gobble, gobble, not to be.. that..gobble, gobble, gobble, is the question. Gobble, gobble, gobble...And, here is my understudy. Chicken Little. (Starts crowing.)

DIRK : Hank...I like that! Hank, (Following him off.) You can use that! Act two! MacBeth comes in like a turkey. You'll be great! Hank? Hank?

COMEDY SCENES

ACTRESS / ACTOR

MAN AND WIFE AT HOME WATCHING TV.

HUSB : Well, I've got the new remote. I hope it works better than the old one.

WIFE : Well, what could I say to her? I felt truly helpless.
(He is pressing the buttons.)

HUSB : Nothing. Nothing. Please work. Please. I don't believe it.

WIFE : I mean, I barely even know her sister. I've met her once and that was well over six years ago.

HUSB : This is not working! Damn it! I don't believe this. Honey, the new remote is on the fritz.

WIFE : Oh, you. It can't be. Here! Let me try.

HUSB : Why? If it doesn't work when I press it, -

WIFE : Maybe, you're holding it wrong. It's the angle. Give it to me.
(He does. She tries. Nothing happens.)
Well, obviously, they sold you a bad one. Did you check the batteries?

HUSB : Of course. First thing. Here, hand it over. (She does.) This is so frustrating.

WIFE : Maybe, it's not the remote. Maybe, it's the set. So, her sister, who lives in Chicago, goes to visit her in Montana. I mean, anyone who moves out to Montana, should not be surprised by marital difficulties.

HUSB : I'm not giving up. You see, when you point it like this...nothing. Why doesn't it work?

WIFE : I'm sure that her husband was not riding 20 miles to the next ranch, just to pick up a cup of flour.
(He presses the remote in her direction.)

WIFE : And, now the local weather. Today, our high reached 41 degrees. About five degrees above normal, and tomorrow will again be warmer than expected...

HUSB : Honey?

WIFE : Now, let's look ahead to the five day forecast for Spokane and the three town area. The strange and yet unexplained atmospheric disturbances are still plaguing the Northwest.

HUSB : Let me click this off.

WIFE : (Without missing a beat.) Not only buffalo roam. And when there's nothing to separate your husband from your sister, but you and 100 head of homely-looking cattle and you -

HUSB : Honey, why did you just give me the weather report?

WIFE : Huh? The what report?

HUSB : The weather report.

WIFE : The weather report? I never did any such thing. (He presses the remote.)

HUSB : On! Channel 10!

WIFE : (She is now Humprey Bogart in Casablanca.) Of all the gin joints...in all the world, she had to walk into mine.

HUSB : She's doing Casablanca! (He runs his hand in front of her eyes.) Honey?

WIFE : Play it, Sam. If you can take it, so can I.

HUSB : She's a movie! Beverly, can you hear me?

WIFE : (Singing) You must remember this, a kiss is just a kiss.

HUSB : What else? Channel 6.

WIFE : This sucks, Beavis. If you don't shut up I'm going to squash your nads...Bon Jovi blows...

HUSB : By God. It's happening. My wife...is a television set!

WIFE : Shut up, fart knocker. This is cool.

HUSB : A re-run. The Playboy Channel?

WIFE : (Her face contorts and she makes sounds of raw passion.)

HUSB : Damn. Pay for View. No picture, just sound. It's making me hungry. Channel 22. The Food Channel...It's scrambled... What else would it be! CHANNEL SURF! (He runs the channel gamut and she reacts with one word bursts and poses.) Look at her go! I've heard of channeling, but this is channeling. Fantastic. Whoa, girl, whoa. Let's settle down.

WIFE : I slept with ten men in one week and then I also slept with their teen-age sons. Why not?

HUSB : SALLY JESSE RAPHAEL.

WIFE : Now, they all want to leave home and -

HUSB : SHUT UP! SHUT UP! MUTE! Mute. My wife is on mute. Thank you, God!

(Wife is chatting silently.)
Bring this back to the store?   Never!   But, how long can it last?   The energy fields or whatever.   Sun spots.   I love it. She seems to be enjoying herself.   But, is this fair to her? What if she has things to do?   Who cares?   This is better. This is heaven.   But, I must tell her.   I have to tell her.   (He presses button.)

WIFE : Three people on one ranch?   How many chores are there?
HUSB : Honey,   I'm sorry to interrupt, but I have something truly incredible to (He begins to ring like a telephone.)
WIFE : Bobby, what are you doing?   Bobby?
(He continues to ring.)
Bob, stop being foolish.   You sound ridiculous.
(She raises his arm and a voice comes out of his mouth.)
HUSB : Hello?   Hello?   Beverly?   Are you home?   Can you hear me?
WIFE : (Talking into Bob's elbow.)
Nancy?   Is this Nancy?   Nancy?   What are you doing coming out of my husband?   Is this a trick?
HUSB : Beverly?   I can hardly hear you.   It's a bad connection.
WIFE : (Speaking into her husbands ear.)
How's this? Nancy?   It's Bev.
HUSB : That's much better.   Bev, I've been meaning to call for days. Can you talk or are you busy with Bob?
WIFE : (She stares at her husband for a while.)   Not really.   But, hold on.   I'm taking the phone into another room.   (As she and he exit.)   So, tell me what happened on the ranch.   Did the lawyer finally call?   I'm just dying to know.

A YOUNG ACTOR'S PHONE CALL TO HOME.

BERT : Mom, how are you? I'm fine.

MOM : Bert, how are you? Herb, it's Bert. Long distance.

BERT : I said I'm fine. Can't you hear me? How's Dad?

MOM : Swell. Standing right here. Waving. How's New York? The Big Apple? As exciting as they say?

BERT : Well...

MOM : Have you found work?

BERT : Sure.

MOM : That's wonderful. Herb, our actor son has found work.

BERT : Four shifts a week in a great restaurant. Tips aren't tops. But at least I get to eat and I've met some very important people in show business.

MOM : Herb, in less than a month, he's already met very important people in show business. Isn't that wonderful?

BERT : Yeah. They all work at the restaurant.

MOM : Well, it's an honest living.

BERT : Possibly. Ma, this isn't collect. So, without being crass, may I move on? Equity. Actor's Equity.

MOM : Actor's what? Is that a slogan, dear?

BERT : No, it's a union. A very important union. I know I must have mentioned it many times before. Didn't I?

MOM : Really? Well, what about it?

BERT : Either I join, or I don't work professionally anywhere in the universe. Most parts I can't even audition for. It's the business. I have no choice.

MOM : Dad's a union man. We understand. You must join.

BERT : Exactly. Okay, I'm going to say it once. Because, I know you care. $800. And 37 for six months dues. And I swear I'll pay it back....Ma?...Ma?

MOM : Pay whom back?

BERT : Every cent...and it won't be long, I promise...Ma?

MOM : Well...are you sure it's very necessary?

BERT : Would I humble myself if it wasn't?

MOM : Hold on. I'll ask your father. $837? It's for some actors union...He must join...Bert, your Dad says,...Was that a yes? Yes, it's a yes. Is that a yes? It's a full yes.

BERT : Oh, thanks, Dad. Thanks, Mom. You're both so great.

MOM : We'll send the check off tomorrow. Have you had a chance to call Uncle Milton in Philadelphia?

BERT : Ma, no. But, I will. Oh, one more little thing.

MOM : How little?

BERT : Equity means new pictures. Mine stink.

MOM : ...I don't think so.

BERT : Graduation Day shots don't cut it. I need a "look." I'm a product. Professional headshots.

MOM : Professional whatshots?

BERT : One session; prints, mailing, follow-up. The whole kit and kaboodle a smidge under, a reasonable $700. Ma?

MOM : ...Did you say $700? Is that on top of the first $800?

BERT : $839.

MOM : $837. $700 on top of 837? Am I hearing right?

BERT : Ma, for God's sakes, it's venture capital. And, I'm the venture! It's money in the bank. Ma?

MOM : Hold on...Herb? He's your son, too! Did I say "Go for it. Follow your stupid star?" No, you did! Now, look! He's not a son! He's a sinkhole.

BERT : I heard that! Ma, you saw me in Kismet. Was I fabulous? Arsenic and Old Lace? Better than Cary Grant and he died a billionaire. Yes or no? He paid back everyone.

MOM : But, not us.

BERT : It's $700, plus 837. Big deal.

MOM : Bert, actor or not, it is time you took responsibility-

BERT : Is Dad there? May I please talk to Dad?

MOM : You can't.

BERT : Why not?

MOM : Because, he just ran out the door.

BERT : Oh, great.

MOM : WHAT HAPPENED TO THE MONEY WE SENT LAST MONTH?

BERT : $100? Ma, I'm in New York.

MOM : Well, I'm not.

BERT : Do you think I want this? But, what can I do? I'm gifted.

MOM : Do what most people your age do. Support yourself!

BERT : Oh, must you make this personal?

MOM : You're a son. Not a charity.

BERT : I resent that. I AM a charity!

MOM : God damn it! We are not made of money.

BERT : Ma, please, don't curse. It's not motherly.

MOM : You punk! We're still paying off your goddamned college!

BERT : Don't blame me. I never wanted to go.

MOM : And for $1537, I can curse all I want.

BERT : Hey, if you're broke at your age, it's your fault. You should have planned better and drank less.

MOM : What did you say? You rotten little bastard! I'll come to New York and wring your ungrateful neck.

BERT : Oh, that's nice.

MOM : Pride, Bert. Pride. We raised you to have pride.

BERT : I have tons of pride. But, I am man enough not to allow it to interfere with my life! I'm an actor and I need money. So get used to it. I am.

MOM : And, I'm your mother, Bert. So, get used to no!

BERT : Fine. Okay, so, where do we stand? I mean, economically?

MOM : $837 and not a red cent more. Goodbye.

BERT : ...But, what about my pictures?

MOM : TAKE A PENCIL THAT YOU SHOULD BE SELLING, AND DRAW THEM.
(She hangs up.)

BERT : Okay...They get the usual thank you note. $700 to go. Let's see? Grandma? Mmmm. She's worth a call. Where did I put the number for the nursing home? Nuts. Hey, Charlie? Do you have a grandmother? I think mine may be in a coma. Charlie? Charlie? (Bert exits.)

INSPIRATION.
(Adapted from Claptrap.)

SARA : (Dashing on.) Sam, put down the damned tea and listen.
SAM : Hi, Honey. What's up?
SARA : Brace yourself! You're going to meet my mother.
SAM : Oh, like hell I am. No way. Waitress!
SARA : But, Sam, something terrible has happened.
SAM : Oh, God. No! You lost your job?
SARA : No. My stepfather has passed on.
SAM : Oh, wow. Sara, that's sad. He was so young.
SARA : 85.
SAM : Well, compared to someone even older.
SARA : And, mother is deeply upset.
SAM : Why? That he lived that long?
SARA : Okay, it's true. She hated him. But, Sam, now that he's gone, her love for the bastard is abloom. And, she's left it to me to make the arrangements, and I think its time mother met you, isn't it? And, I've never arranged a funeral and I don't know where to begin.
SAM : Well, don't look at me, because I'm not going.
SARA : And, she wants a beautiful and expensively tasteful ceremony.
SAM : Money down the drain. Hand it to charity.
SARA : Floral arrangements. Music. Even a minister. It could total well over $6,000.
SAM : That's- HOW MUCH?
SARA : $6,000.
SAM : I'll do it!
SARA : Oh, thank you, Sam. You'll attend the funeral?
SAM : Attend it? God damn it, baby, I'll run it!
SARA : What? Oh, no! Oh, no.
SAM : Oh, yes, baby! I'm your man! I can do it!
SARA : You? Sam, you're not qualified.
SAM : Why? What can it take? You roll him in. You roll him out.
SARA : But, don't you need a license?
SAM : I can drive. And, I had six years of college.

SARA : As a freshman.

SAM : College is college. Let me do it, Sara. Please? Why am I not as good as the next fellow? Sure, he can be an undertaker, but not me. I'm not good enough. Thank you!

SARA : I've never said that. But, it's $6,000.

SAM : I'll do it for $5,850. Last offer! What are you going to do? Put it out for bids? I'm ready. I'm eager. Give me a suit. A box! A pulpit. We'll roll.

SARA : Sam, I've never seen you like this.

SAM : I've never been like this. Listen to me. You think I can't say "Good morning, widow. Take my arm, for I am strong." and shove a stiff into a hearse? Come on, kid! One man's demise is another's prize! Roll with me, baby. Roll. That's all I ask. Love your man and back him.

SARA : By golly, Sam, you're right! And if you can do it, so can I.

SAM : Yes! That's the spirit. It's a partnership.

SARA : Sam and Saras Sayonara Suite! Oh, I'm so into this.

SAM : It can work. It will work. Money for your honey.

SARA : But, where? Where can we go on such short notice?

SAM : Right downstairs from where I live.

SARA : In the Chinese laundry? That can only sit twelve.

SAM : No, silly! Across the street. The vacant store.

SARA : Mr. Lightning's Chicken and Ribs? A splendid choice.

SAM : Closed a week. They'll still have chairs.

SARA : And a faint aroma of greasy fried chicken.

SAM : We'll call it incense.

SARA : I'll knit curtains!

SAM : And, you doubted me. You thought you were in love with a loser. But, sweetknees, I've got it!

SARA : I'll design a logo.

SAM : Great idea. You're cooking now!

SARA : Crossed shovels! And I'll sing. I love to sing.

SAM : You'll sing?

SARA : "Swing low, sweet chariot, coming for to carry him hoooome."

SAM : Sara...

SARA : We'll need a name.

SAM : I'll need a check.

SARA : How about...From Birth to Earth? No? Death and Things? Mourning, spelled with a "U", Noon and Night?

SAM : Too literate.

SARA : It's Your Funeral?

SAM : I love that. It's catchy and it tells a story.

SARA : Buried Treasure? Dead, Bath and Beyond? Hold it! THE LUCKY STIFF!

SAM : Sensational. That'll bring 'em in.

SARA : Oh, how about this? Tape the memorials and go on Cable TV. The Funeral Channel. Death, 24 hours a day.

SAM : Sara...calm down.

SARA : We'll franchise and be in Malls. Counseling for the bereaved and SINGLES WEEKENDS for the survivors.

SAM : Sara-

SARA : But, nothing tacky. All high class. We will not pander.

SAM : We won't need to.

SARA : I'll quit my job.

SAM : Sara, let's not go overboard.

SARA : I've never been so excited. Oh, haroo! Haroo! A few moments ago we sat moping over a cup of tea.

SAM : Hopelessly lost. I, not only not wanting to meet your Mom, but anyone else, as well. But now...

SARA : We are ready to go to a phone. A telephone. How many people can say that?

SAM : To tell your Mom that her prayers have been answered.

SARA : It's the American dream! Pay the check.

SAM : The American dream. Oh God, I wish we were immigrants.

SARA : Maybe someday we will be. Let's go! We have work to do. (They exit.) This is a cause for celebration! Sam and Sara have found their niche and are on their way to success.

A COUPLE THAT'S BEEN TOGETHER FOR TOO LONG.

KEN : Oh, Lord! Here's to us! Here's to another 35 years of "Oh, aren't they cute?"

BARB : Ken, you're drunk! And I don't like it.

KEN : LAY OFF ME, BARBIE! I'M SICK OF YOUR GRIEF!

BARB : And, I'm sick of living my life with a plastic alcoholic!

KEN : Well, what do you want? Nag! Nag! Nag! Oh, if America only knew. You wouldn't be on a pedestal. You would be on a broom. You're making me crazy. Just what do you want?

BARB : Oh, I don't think you really want to know. Do you, Ken?

KEN : Spit it out! Say what's on your mind. God knows, Barbie, there's not room for very much.

BARB : Not Barbie. Barbra! How many times have I told you? I am not a mid-western teenage air head. For several years I've been a very sophisticated and highly motivated astronautess cum congressional aide. And you know it.

KEN : So what? You still can't read.

BARB : And you still can't-

KEN : Can't what? Can't what, Barbara?

BARB : Ken, can we just change the subject?

KEN : No, Barbie. What can't I do? What do you want?

BARB : Ken, please! Don't push me.

KEN : Say it! Say it! Say it!

BARB : I'd rather not.

KEN : Then I will. In plain English; you want a boyfriend with balls.

BARB : Ken! Genitalia!

KEN : Spheres are spheres. And, let me ask you this, Babs, with all due respect, what would you do if I had them?

BARB : What other girls do. I would describe them to my friends. It's not much, but it's better than nothing.

KEN : Oh, Barbie, don't you think it torments me to know that the only way I'll ever get a pubic hair is with a paintbrush?

BARB : Ken, don't. Please.

KEN   : And for a lousy extra two cents worth of plastic,-

BARB : You could have been a stud.

KEN   : King Ken. Instead, I am what I am.

BARB : Anatomically bereft. And the irony of it all. We want to have children! But instead, it's children who want to have us.

KEN   : Barbie, what are we? What have we become?

BARB : It's humiliating. How many other forty year olds weigh 12 ounces and move like Frankenstein? Only us!

KEN   : We're useless. Overrated and oversold. We've never developed our full potential. We've never grown.

BARB : And yet, we're popular. We're beloved.

KEN   : Yes, we're beloved. But, by whom? Sticky-fingered eight year olds with the attention spans of a hummingbird.

BARB : It's not gratifying. We're intelligent. We're involved.

KEN   : We have minds. We have intellects. Just once, why can't we appear on Meet the Press?

BARB : Or Biography?

KEN   : Barbie, I...I want you to know that lately I've been thinking about taking my own life.

BARB : And, what's stopped you?

KEN   : I don't have one! I pray they develop a Suicidal Ken doll. Kids would love it. Let me end it. Let me go to the attic with dignity.

BARB : Ken, stop it! Stop it.
(She smacks him in the face in Doll-like slow motion.)
You're a doll! Act like one! Be happy.

KEN   : No. I'm just so sick of the pathetic charade.

BARB : Come on, where's the old Ken? Where's the Ken that set the standard? We all grow old.

KEN   : We won't. Even if we were lucky enough to die, it'll still take us 30,000 years to decompose.

BARB : Put down that bottle, Ken, and listen to me. Listen to me and remember this...

KEN   : Oh, no. Good grief. Don't sing.

BARB : Remember, always remember...

KEN   : I hate it when you sing.

BARB : (Into song. Any song. "When You Walk through a Storm." Or "She Loves Me, Yeah, Yeah, Yeah." Whatever strikes you either as ridiculous or appropriate and it should turn into a duet, as they dance off; stiff legged, but proud.)

BACKSTAGE, FIVE HOURS BEFORE OPENING NIGHT.

BERT : Now listen, Polly. Are you listening?

POLLY : Yes, Bert.

BERT : I don't want you to be upset. We're all under a lot of pressure. You, me, everyone.

POLLY : I know that. We're all under a lot of pressure.

BERT : So, if I yell at you?

POLLY : It's not personal.

BERT : Good. This is a low budget production, and even though we're actors and we shouldn't be doing the things we've been doing, with only five hours until opening, is there a choice? FIVE HOURS!

POLLY : Five hours.

BERT : Now, I am laying out my own money for intermission coffee.

POLLY : That's very nice of you.

BERT : Why? BECAUSE EVEN THOUGH I'M BROKE, OUR PRODUCER, THAT FRAUDULENT PILE OF PUKE, HAS LESS MONEY THAN I DO! DON'T CRY! PLEASE!

POLLY : I'm sorry. But, everyone is shouting at me. Everyone is screaming, all the time.

BERT : That's okay, Polly. That's the way it's supposed to be. Now, while I finish painting, you go to the store and buy it. The coffee. Can you do that?

POLLY : Of course, I can. I can buy coffee.

BERT : Good. Thank you, Polly. You're wonderful.

POLLY : What kind?

BERT : What kind?

POLLY : Of coffee?

BERT : DON'T ASK ME WHAT KIND!

POLLY : But, Bert, I don't drink coffee.

BERT : NEITHER DO I, YOU IDIOT! Don't cry. Don't cry.

POLLY : Why?

BERT : Why shouldn't you cry?

POLLY : Why don't you drink coffee? Is it bad for your nerves?

BERT : No. Yes. No. I CAN'T THINK!

POLLY : Tomorrow, I'm going to bake cookies. Chocolate chip. and at act break, I'm going to sell them and share the money.

BERT : That's swell. Polly, may I hug you?

POLLY	:	Why?
BERT	:	Nothing heavy. Just…for luck.
		(He embraces her and doesn't let go.)
BERT	:	Is this your first show?
POLLY	:	Yes.
BERT	:	First you've worked on or the first you've seen?
POLLY	:	I saw two in High School and I loved them both.
BERT	:	Good. I want you to know that even though what we're doing is a play, it has nothing at all to do with theater.
POLLY	:	It doesn't?
BERT	:	No. And, I LOVE YOU! God, I love you.
POLLY	:	Bert, you're squeezing me.
BERT	:	Yes. Because, you're so innocent, clean, and untalented. Save me, Polly Pittman. Save me from my life.
POLLY	:	Bert, no. Please. It's wrong.
BERT	:	You're wrong. It's right. You are mine. Young, warm and so sweet. Warm and sweet and soft and sweet and warm.
POLLY	:	Bert, stop kissing me.
BERT	:	I can't.
POLLY	:	Bert, you're eight years older.
BERT	:	I'll lie about my age! Polly, after last night's rehearsal, I threw up and then drew up my will. You're in it.
POLLY	:	I am?
BERT	:	You get it all. Sheets, pillow cases. Everything I own.
POLLY	:	That's kind.
BERT	:	Just say that you like me. Give me you. Please?
POLLY	:	Bert, I just don't like you. I love you!
BERT	:	No? You do? You don't?
POLLY	:	And I think your portrayal of Philippe, a homosexual Archbishop is brilliant, and I love you. And, I want to move in with you. I thought you loved me, but I wasn't sure. I want to marry you. I've written to my mother and told her all about you.
BERT	:	Really?
POLLY	:	And when she gets here next week, and meets you, she'll approve. She married an older man, too. He's dead, but he smoked.
BERT	:	Polly, hold on. I don't think I clearly defined my terms.
POLLY	:	Love has no terms.

BERT : You'd be surprised. I was thinking along the lines of a deep, caring and great physical love. I call it orgasm without ownership. Intense, honest, but potentially brief and leaving very few detectable scars. There is a big age difference. And I have one room!

POLLY : I don't care. We'll stand at different times. I love you and that's it!

BERT : Fine. But, don't love me openly. Because, once you start and I know it, then it just turns to crap. So, please, let me love you and mind your own business. Fair? I think so.

POLLY : That won't work. That's not the woman that I am. I cannot love my man in secret.

BERT : Just go to the goddamned store! OKAY?

POLLY : You're angry. You're afraid of commitment.

BERT : No. Listen, can we discuss this later? Darling?

POLLY : Do you love me? Yes or no? Do you? Do you?

BERT : Of course. Yes. Would I just say that? Coffee?

POLLY : Coffee. Coffee for my love.

BERT : And a receipt. Hurry, sweetheart, we have to finish the set.
(She dashes off.)
JESUS CHRIST! Her goddamned mother. Shit! Charlie?
CHARLIE?
(Walking off.)
WHERE THE HELL ARE THE BRUSHES? WHERE THE HELL AM I?

A WAITER FALLS IN LOVE WITH A FEMALE CUSTOMER.

WAIT : Hi, everything...okay? How was your Veal...Chop?

LOIS : Okay. A little dry. But, otherwise...fine. Yes?

WAIT : May I get you...anything else?

LOIS : No...no, thank you.

WAIT : I only ask, because I want you to be happy. How about dessert? You can't tell me you're counting calories, not with a body like yours.

LOIS : Mmm, I'll wait to order until my friend comes back.

WAIT : Your friend? The guy? Say, is he your boyfriend? He can't be. Not him? No way.

LOIS : I beg your pardon?

WAIT : The guy who went to the phone? The short guy? With the bad sweater? He's not your boyfriend?

LOIS : No. Actually-I really don't think-

WAIT : Well, that's a relief. May I sit down?

LOIS : Here?

WAIT : Sure. Just for a minute. (He sits next to her.)

LOIS : Is this really appropriate? You ARE a waiter?

WAIT : Aren't we all. Hi, my name is Dirk. Thank you for speaking to me, not as a servant, but as a man. A real man. And you're Lois. I overheard and remembered. Lois, from the looks of things we probably don't have that much time to get acquainted, what do you think? So, let me just say this: You are one hell of a woman! And I'd like to ball you. Make love? Give it some thought. Okay?

LOIS : I should slap you. Are you crazy?

WAIT : Only about you.

LOIS : I don't believe this! You are way out of line...

WAIT : Oh, don't tell me you've never flirted with a waiter.

LOIS : Of course, I have! Many times. And I'm proud of it.

WAIT : Or a waiter with you? A look, a little glance, a smile. It's restaurant etiquette. You've done it, I've done it. It's fun and whets the appetite. But as of tonight, I have outgrown the note on the napkin, phone number frustration. I throw caution to the winds.

LOIS : What exactly do you have in mind?

WAIT : KISS ME!

LOIS : I will not!

WAIT : Kiss me, customer! I'm on my break. One kiss.

LOIS : Sir, that's my knee you are touching.

WAIT : No, it's our knee. Don't reject me. What will it take? More coffee? Free dessert? Oh, Lois, you don't know what it's like. Every night, other couples holding hands. Cooing. NEVER ME! I want some, too. And, tonight, when you… you…Your order, your napkin tucking, your elbows on the table. You are sensational.

LOIS : Okay. I cannot fight your logic. Have me. Right here. Under the table. Now.

(They dive under the table and roll around.)

WAIT : Here? Do you really mean it?

LOIS : Totally. Okay, so you're merely a waiter, but you can do better. A haircut, some work with weights, a second job and some day you can finish high school, and I'll be waiting.

WAIT : I have plans to go back.

LOIS : I've always wanted, dreamed, no, longed for a man with a damp cloth hanging from his belt, to crash into my life; to care, cavort and cater to my every whim. You're it!

WAIT : Oh, Lois! I love you! I want to devour you!

LOIS : But, first, there is one thing you must know.

WAIT : Nothing matters! Nothing.

LOIS : If we do it, or any part of said "it"…no tip.

WAIT : No tip? Are you mad? You don't mean that.

LOIS : I mean every word.

WAIT : Lois, you don't know what you're saying. No tip?

LOIS : No gratuity! It's me or the money.

WAIT : DON'T MAKE ME CHOOSE!

LOIS : Me or the money.

WAIT : Oh, Lord. I want you both.

LOIS : Dirk, if you love me, prove it!

WAIT : You bitch! Okay, damn it! You may be the greatest thing that's ever happened to me, but, baby, you're still not 15%. Love comes, love goes…but, double the tax is the stuff of life. The decision is difficult. But, gratuities are celestial and Lois, I choose my faith.

(They get out from beneath the table.)

LOIS : We'll never know what could have been. But, we clearly know what really is...A farewell handshake?

WAIT : Sure. Lois, as much as I'd like to stay with you forever, I have another table...Oh, Wednesday? Fish fry.

LOIS : I like a nice piece of fish.

WAIT : So, do I. And a potato.

LOIS : Dirk, you made this meal almost special. Too bad we never got to dessert. And, Dirk?

WAIT : Yes?

LOIS : I'd like another glass of water, a re-fill on my coffee, it's cold, and a fresh napkin. Thank you. Oh, hi George! What took you so long?

DINNER FOR TWO.

LOIS : Are you going to pay attention, or aren't you?

FRED : Of course, I'm paying attention.

LOIS : (To the waiter.) Yes, we're finished. Leave the bread. Thank you.

FRED : (To the waiter.) Keep the change.

LOIS : Now, to be frank, Fred, my feelings are not hurt -

FRED : How could they be? Lois, I said you were very good. I enjoyed the show. I paid for dinner. What else?

LOIS : You said my performance was great, but that there were a couple of little things -

FRED : Well, there were. But nothing that -

LOIS : Fred, I don't want to strike you in public. In my performance there are never little things. And I don't need to hear about them even if you think there were.

FRED : Okay, I'm sorry.

LOIS : I don't want our friendship to suffer, but you simply don't know how to speak to a PPA; post performance actress. It takes skill and some sensitivity.

FRED : I -

LOIS : May I finish? In theatre, there is no such thing as FCC; Friendly Constructive Criticism.

FRED : How was I to know? I'm sorry.

LOIS : All criticism is unfriendly and destructive.

FRED : I mean't no harm.

LOIS : So, dump FCC and learn what counts; CCA.

FRED : CCA? What in the world is CCA?

LOIS : Constant Constructive Adoration. This simple and pleasant approach to actors can change your life.

FRED : Really?

LOIS : Sure. So, listen as I teach you the language of Art. Three words: "You were wonderful." And that's it in a nutshell. "You were wonderful." May I hear them please? Now!

FRED : Lois, really.

LOIS : Fred, don't aggravate me. May I hear the words?

FRED : You were wonderful.

LOIS : Again.

FRED : You were wonderful.
LOIS : Disgraceful. Is that the best you can do?
FRED : What do you want from me? Should I play a bugle?
LOIS : Exactly. Put life into it. Give it guts.
FRED : Okay. But this is the last time. You were wonderful.
LOIS : Pathetic. Are you thrilled with me or the tablecloth?
FRED : Well, it's embarrassing. People can hear.
LOIS : EUREKA! Now, you're catching on. Again. Again.
FRED : You were wonderful.
LOIS : Why are you finding this so difficult?
FRED : You were wonderful. I'm trying. I'm doing my best.
LOIS : Look at me. Hold my hand. And choose one word to emphasize. And the look in your eye? Try awe.
FRED : Lois, you were wonderful.
LOIS : Nice. Very nice. You're starting to get it.
FRED : You were ...wonderful.
LOIS : Richer. Good work. Now, let it sing! Fill the room.
Lois, I saw your performance and you were wonderful.
FRED : Lois, I saw your performance and you were wonderful.
LOIS : Thank you. Would it help if I put my hand on your knee? Call it positive reinforcement.
FRED : That might -
(She places her hand on his thigh.)
Oh yes, you were wonderful. Better than everybody. What an actress. What a performance. God, you were so good. Lois. Lois. Lois.
LOIS : Better, Fred, better. Now, don't lose the edge, because we are ready to go. This is more difficult. ALR. Actress Leaving Restaurant. Hold the mood. Hold it. Gaze at me. Gaze.
FRED : I'm gazing. You were wonderful.
LOIS : You stand first; good, nice stand, now, smile at me.
(He smiles.)
Too big. Smaller, gentler; "I am in awe of you, and I want people to see me with you." smile. Hold that pose. Nice.
FRED : You were really wonderful. Wonderful. Top notch. Great.
LOIS : Good. Let people realize that I am about to rise and they can get a real long look at me, if they're lucky. Okay? Here I come. I'm standing.
(She rises.)

FRED : I can sense people watching. How long do we stand here? My legs are cramping.

LOIS : Shut up. Gaze at me. Let them wonder: "Is he going home with her? Is he going to spend the night?" Okay, deep breath. Now we leave.

(Walking through the audience.)

Walk. Slowly. Good. You first, head up, pretend to know someone and nod in their direction; good. Now, I sweep past you. I walk straight ahead, too important and splendid to acknowledge anyone. DON'T TRIP!

FRED : Sorry. Did that spill? So sorry.

(They are outside.)

LOIS : Good job. I'm proud.

FRED : Thanks.

LOIS : Now, comes the really hard part. Since, we can't afford a taxi, should we walk home or take the subway?

(They laugh and skip away.)

THE DOCTORS OFFICE.

DOC : Adele, send Miss Muller in.

JUDY : Oh, Doctor Sprice, I am so glad you could see me. I'm having a breakdown. I'm going insane.

DOC : Now, Judy, stay calm. Relax.

JUDY : I can't relax. I mean I try to, but it's impossible.

DOC : Well, what seems to be your latest problem?

JUDY : Two nights ago, about 4 A.M., I woke up and started...I started...Oh, Doctor...I...

DOC : Started doing what? Tell me.

JUDY : Telling jokes! I don't know why. Three or four in a row. And then it passed and I felt fine. But, the next day it started happening again. Jokes from out of nowhere.

DOC : Hmmm. Is anyone else in your family telling jokes?

JUDY : No. Just me. And, I'm not the kind of person that tells jokes. I find most jokes either offensive or inane or both.

DOC : Well, is there a fever? Nausea? Or-

JUDY : Doc! Doc! It's coming! It's...I can feel it! HEEEERES JUDY! Hi, folks. Say, did you hear about the Polack who spent five hours trapped inside a revolving door? He was looking for a knob. These are the jokes, folks. Ra ba boom! (She regains her composure.)

DOC : This could be serious.

JUDY : And I'm a respectable woman. I teach Freshman English!

DOC : How much time between episodes?

JUDY : Like labor pains, they're coming faster. I'm fine for an hour, even two, and then I may do six or seven in a row.

DOC : With introductions or without?

JUDY : With-Oh! Here it comes again. Here comes another one!

DOC : Try to suppress it. Fight back. Clench your teeth.

JUDY : I can't! It's like hiccups. HEEEEEEERES JUDY! I wired flowers for my mother-in-law, but she found the fuse. What's a rotisserie? A Ferris Wheel for chickens. I'VE NEVER EVEN HEARD THAT JOKE! Please, help me.

DOC : We'll...We'll have to-

JUDY : HEEEEEEERES JUDY! Thank you, you're beautiful. You know when age creeps up on a woman? When she

62

marries an older man. But, seriously, I once entered a beauty contest and was fined $100. Nice suit. Gestapo? Doctor, my- Reincarnation! I know a waiter who died and who came back as a clock and still complained, "I only have two hands."

DOC : Hold your breath! Make fists. Fists, Judy. Fists.

JUDY : I've had five husbands, two were mine. To err is human, but it feels divine. Money! If it pays to be ignorant, how come you're always broke?

DOC : Judy, can you hear me?

JUDY : Of- HEEEERE'S JUDY! Thank you, you're a great crowd. But, seriously, some candidates are called favorite sons. Why don't they ever finish the sentence? So, this man comes home from work and his wife says to him: Melvin, you're a pedophile. And he says: My, what a big word for a ten year old. YES! You have to love it. Anybody here from Pittsburgh?...
(She catches her breath and wipes the sweat from her face.)
I'm okay. I'm okay. It passed...Oh God, Oh God.

DOC : You poor woman. I'm sorry you didn't get to me sooner.

JUDY : Is there anything you can do? Put me out. Give me a shot. Next month is my twentieth high school reunion. I CAN'T GO THERE LIKE THIS! Doc, I'm possessed! Is this psychological? Have I lost my mind?

DOC : No. I don't think it's psychological. I think it's viral.

JUDY : Viral? You mean...it's contagious?

DOC : Judy, think, and be truthful. Besides the joke telling, in the past few days have you had any sudden urges to pretend that you were opening a door?

JUDY : I don't think so.

DOC : How about smelling an imaginary flower?

JUDY : No...No. But, wait! This morning I do think I recall standing at the flagpole in the school yard and raising an imaginary flag...Doc, what does it all mean?

DOC : Judy, I think your husband should be present.

JUDY : I can take it! Tell me the worst.

DOC : Judy, these joke outbursts may just be the beginning; the terrible incubation of stages of...Mime Disease.

JUDY : Mime Disease?

DOC : It started last year in Maine and it's been spreading throughout the country. It's believed to be caused by a tick that lives on comedians. In some cases it's fatal. Not to those who have it, but to those who live with them.

JUDY : No. I don't want Mime disease. It's not fair. I'm too young. I don't smoke! I don't drink! I-

DOC : Judy, Judy, what are you doing?
(Judy is going through some silent machinations.)
Oh, dear God! You're peeling a banana!
(He can put on gloves and a face mask.)
Follow me. I want to get you out of here and away from any other patients. (On his intercom.)
Miss Gruber, I have an emergency. I'll call you from the hospital. (She follows him and "slips" on the banana peel.)
Oh, that was good. This could mean quarantine.
(She is now doing lots of standard "Mime" stuff. They exit.)

TWO GOOD FRIENDS AT HOME, HUNTING FOR A NAME.

YVET : Tom, please, be serious.

TOM : I am serious.

YVET : Like hell. I called you to this meeting for a serious reason. Put down the Vodka.

TOM : (He is drunk.) I am.

YVET : I mean on the table. We've got twenty minutes and I still don't have a name. And all we've done for the last hour is drink! I am not spending $300 on new pictures as long as my name is still Yvette Tuchinsky.

TOM : I agree. I fully agree.

YVET : I don't give a damn what my father-Let me have some of that-says. Now, I love my Dad, but-

TOM : But business is business.

YVET : The name is gone. I hate it. EVITA? Starring Yvette Tuchinsky? It doesn't scan. But, I must get a great one!

TOM : How about Christine Columbus? She explores her roles.

YVET : Not funny! Stop drinking. If you stop, I will.

TOM : Okay, how about, for your Dads sake; lose the name, preserve the initials?

YVET : Huh? Preserve? Oh, I like that. Let's go. Think. Think.

TOM : A place to start.

YVET : It is indeed. (She is drunk.) Hurry. A first name with a Y.

TOM : Yolanda?

YVET : No. Yetta? Yogi! Yokum? Yum-Yum? Yerkle. Yam?

TOM : Yada...Yonder...Yvonne? Yvette!

YVET : Yvette? Oh, that's real progress...Y...Y?

TOM : That's it. Why! Your first name should be Why.

YVET : Why? That's absurd. Who's named Why?

TOM : Who? You've heard of Don Knott? You can be Why Knott?

YVET : Tom, if this is beyond your capabilities, say so. Okay? I will not be trifled with on the most important day of my career. I am being born. Let's focus. Shall we?

TOM : I am doing my best.

YVET : You're drunk!

TOM	: So are you.
YVET	: I am not. GOD! We have to leave in TEN MINUTES!
TOM	: It'll come. Initials. Initials.
YVET	: Something me. Pour. Thank you. Vodka helps. There's inspiration in fermentation. Names. Names.
TOM	: Ideas flow. Y. Go with Y.
	(They wander the room.)
	Yasmine? That's it! Yasmine...Wait. Two initials? Why not use three?
YVET	: Three? Three initials?
TOM	: And spell out a word. YET!
YVET	: Yet? Have you been drinking? (They laugh.) Yet? That's ridiculous. Yoo-Too?
TOM	: Yoo-hoo? You two? You, too? YOO-TOO TUTU!
YVET	: I'm canceling! I am not going. It's my own fault for relying on you and not doing this yesterday.
TOM	: THAT'S IT! The name! Yesterday!
YVET	: Yesterday? That's worse than yoo-hoo. Tutu Who Too.
TOM	: No. No. It's good. You've heard of Tuesday Weld? So, why can't you be Yesterday...Tomorrow?
YVET	: I- Hold it. Say that again. Slowly.
TOM	: Yesterday Tomorrow. Oh, boy. Excellent!
YVET	: I love it. I do. Yesterday Tomorrow. Brilliant.
TOM	: WOW! Shake my hand. Five!
YVET	: What a name! Fantastic. Tom, you are a genius.
TOM	: And your friends can call you...YES!
VYET	: My nickname! Yes, yes, yes. Every time someone agrees on anything, it's publicity for me.
TOM	: Ladies and gentlemen, Yesterday Tomorrow! She sums up what used to be with the excitement of what hasn't even happened yet.
YVET	: I love it. I do. So, will Dad. Where's my makeup? Yesterday Tomorrow...Yesterday Tomorrow. Who would have thought of anything so unique...but the two of us?
TOM	: She may have been born Yesterday...
YVET	: But, you can still call me Tomorrow! Tom, I owe you. Dinner. One big dinner or two cheap lunches.

TOM : Lunches.

YVET : Finally me. I am born! A star is born. A quick toast?

TOM : It's empty.

YVET : We'll buy one on the way. We'll celebrate. 100 prints.

TOM : 100 prints.

YVET : 1,000 prints. What a load off my back. How I worried. My Dad- Oh, screw him. He's my stepfather.

TOM : You're brilliant. I'm brilliant.

YVET : We're both brilliant. So, why can't we earn a living? (They both laugh hysterically.)

TOM : We will, darling, we will. Turn off the lights?

YVET : No. Leave them on! Lights up! Lights on! When, I come home I want lights. It's been dark for too long. So, what do you say, my boy? Yesterday Tomorrow is going to take some pictures. Thousands and thousands.

TOM : I feel good.

YVET : Me, too. Confident and strong. Whoops. Confident and strong. (They collide, laugh and stagger off.)

A REUNION AND AN OFFER IN A MAN'S APARTMENT.

WALT : Franny.

FRAN : Walt.

WALT : Come in. Come in. It's been a long time.

FRAN : Indeed, it has. You look...well.

WALT : Thanks. You look...great. What do you think of the apartment? Huh? Huh? I fixed it up.

FRAN : You did?

WALT : Well, the furniture's the same, but I swept. Yes. And, look. It's a painting. Surreal.

FRAN : It certainly is.

WALT : Do you know where I got it? I found it in the gutter.

FRAN : Where? On top of the artist?

WALT : And, as I said, sit down, please, I've been cleaning on a regular basis. Because I wanted you to see the new me without rats.

FRAN : Well, I didn't know you'd been dating. Small joke.

WALT : Franny, I took your advice. Because how you live is who you are. It's all a matter of pride.
(She is pointing and staring.)
What? What?

FRAN : ROACH!

WALT : No? I don't believe it! -

FRAN : ON YOUR SHOE! KILL IT. STEP ON IT!

WALT : I CAN'T! I am so embarrassed. I don't believe this!

FRAN : I do.

WALT : Shoo, roach, shoo. Not my shoe, you go shoo! Go! Oh, man!

FRAN : Kill it. Don't expect it to surrender.

WALT : I can't kill it! I'm a Buddhist.

FRAN : ...Since when?

WALT : Last month. It's mail order.
(To the roach on his shoe.)

WALT : Bad kharma! Bad kharma! I swear to you. I swear. I haven't seen a bug here in six months and as soon as you come in...It's as if they were tapping my phone. She's coming over, let's mobilize. So, where were we?

FRAN : Walt, for God's sakes, it's standing there like a deer!

WALT : It's not a deer! It's a little...thing. And...now, it's going. See? There it goes. Bye.

FRAN : This is truly revolting.

WALT : FORGET THE ROACH!!! Now, as I told you on the phone,

FRAN : And very excitedly.

WALT : I have decided to embark on a totally new venture.

FRAN : That's- (Looking above her head.) SPIDER!

WALT : Where? Unbelievable! Look at that. Spiders are harmless.

FRAN : Not black widows!

WALT : It's not a black widow. It's a little house spider. Don't worry about it. It's just dangling. It won't fall.

FRAN : I hope not.

WALT : Now, let me tell you; will you stop squirming? I can't talk to you if you squirm.

FRAN : Do they bite?

WALT : No. Franny-

FRAN : What? Whatever it is, hurry.

WALT : This is my exciting news.

FRAN : Please tell me, before I'm swallowed.

WALT : Frannie, after much thought, I'm thinking about opening a restaurant.

FRAN : ......You?

WALT : Yes. Is that a hot idea, or what? Now, you know I'm an excellent business man-

FRAN : Since when? I never knew that.

WALT : How could you? I never had a business! But, I'm very good with people, and when my hair grows back-

FRAN : A fly. Look! Two flies!

WALT : So what? Something exotic. Like Mexican. Or maybe even Austro-Hungarian. While I'm in the kitchen, I'll need a hostess.

FRAN : And another roach! AND AN ANT!

WALT : WHERE? OH, JESUS! They must have fumigated in my neighbors apartment! That's it! They fumigate. I get the overflow. It's like I'm accepting refugees.

FRAN : This is disgusting.

WALT : I really do apologize. This is atypical of my life-style.

FRAN : Forget the restaurant, open a zoo!

WALT : MY PLACE IS SPOTLESS! Now, I have visited a couple of prime locations-

FRAN : Oh, God! A water bug! It's huge!

WALT : Where? NO! On my new painting!

FRAN : They eat paint!

WALT : These are not my bugs. Get away from my painting! Get off there, you son of a bitch.

FRAN : Do you mind? (She takes off her shoe.)

WALT : No! No! Don't squash him on the canvas! There he goes. (She starts pursuing the bug around the apartment.)

WALT : I respect all life.

FRAN : So, respect mine. Missed him! Again! Again!

WALT : Watch out for the lamp. I want to start with no more than a dozen tables, my thesis being; if you keep small, you're always filled. People love to wait in line. (Franny is flailing away.) We'll create our own cuisine. And I want you-

FRAN : Another one!

WALT : Another what?

FRAN : Another - AHHHHHH!

WALT : WHAT?

FRAN : A MOUSE!!!

WALT : No! WOW!

FRAN : AND, I'M BAREFOOT! I'M BAREFOOT! GOD! (They are both jumping around.)

FRAN : Give me a broom! It's coming at me!

WALT : All I need is ten grand and that's not a lot. I have a significant, if small part of that myself.

FRAN : So long, Walt. You're on your own!

WALT : Franny, wait! I'm leaving with you.

FRAN : Wait, really nice seeing you. Let's talk again, real soon. (They rush out the door.)

TWO PEOPLE LITERALLY FALLING IN LOVE.

MIKE : Hi, how you doing?

CAROL : How do you think I'm doing tottering on a ledge, ten stories above the cement pavement?

MIKE : Not that well?

CAROL : Good guess. Yes, I'm ending it all.

MIKE : Hey, I buy the gesture. Intense. Go for it.

CAROL : Stay back. Stay away from me! No one is going to stop me.

MIKE : Stop you? Miss, on the contrary. I was coming home from work, looked up; saw you on this ledge, and I said to myself: Man, why didn't I think of that? So, I did.

CAROL : What are you saying?

MIKE : Simply, that thanks to your example, I'm jumping, too.

CAROL : Oh, no. This is my leap. I was here first. Please go.

MIKE : By the way, I'm Mike. And, I will not go. I mean, I will, but not the way I came. And you?

CAROL : Carol, and I don't believe you. It's a cheap trick.

MIKE : No. Honest. I'm here to share the experience.

CAROL : Oh, this is so unfair! This is my moment. And, I would appreciate some much desired privacy.

MIKE : Privacy? Are you kidding? Look below. Hi, folks! Double feature! Be down in a jiffy.

CAROL : This is the final humiliation. Now, people will think that we're together. No! Wait! Bert, there's another humiliation that's even worse than that one.

MIKE : I'm Mike, and I beg your pardon?

CAROL : The humiliation of being in this God awful scene with you. I hate it! And so do they. Am I right?

MIKE : Carol,-

CAROL : It's Yvette. You know it, I know it and everyone in this classroom knows it. I'm Yvette and I'm leaving this idiotic bilge which pretends to find something Ha-Ha funny in two people killing themselves. I don't! And, if anybody should kill himself, it's the jerk who wrote it. Two losers meeting cute and falling in love, makes me puke. The only thing suicidal about this scene is being in it and I'm out!

MIKE : You're out? How-

CAROL : It's a disgrace. A scene about suicide called Jumping for Joy is CRAP! And, you know it.

MIKE : Yvette, this is incredibly unprofessional-

CAROL : Ladies and gentlemen, classmates, I want to speak for actresses and actors everywhere,

MIKE : Will you shut up?

CAROL : Who are forced to do third rate material written by fourth rate writers who don't give a damn what happens to us. Just get up there and be stupid.

MIKE : I was warned about you. But, I wouldn't listen.

CAROL : Let us all say no to trash! I don't respect this scene, and to do it would be disrespectful of my craft and of myself.

MIKE : And you love both.

CAROL : Therefore, as an artist, a true artist, I owe it to our community to resign. I will not do shit! Bert, jump. The ledge is yours. This actress quits.
(She leaves the stage and the room. He is stuck.)

MIKE : Well...This is...Well, so, I guess the scene is probably over. Uh...now what? Uh, well,...as many of you know, this is my first experience as a director and I think I'll learn from it. I'd like to thank that young actress, Yvette Tuchinsky, for screwing up all my hard work with her disgusting display of selfishness and neuroses.

CAROL : (From outside the room.) IT STINKS! I RAIL AGAINST MEDIOCRITY.

MIKE : Because, I know it would have been damned good.

CAROL : DON'T BET ON IT!

MIKE : And, frankly, right now, I am lost. So, being that I'm lost it follows that I don't know what to do, so I will apologize and leave the stage. The loss is not only mine.

CAROL : IT REEKED! I'M PROUD OF WHAT I'VE DONE!

MIKE : It is also yours. We all know whom to blame.

CAROL : YOU! AND THE SHMUCK WHO WROTE IT.

MIKE : A frightened immature amateur who will never make it in this business and should quit acting class, because deep down she knows, as we all do, that she is a maniac with no discernible talent. A waste of tuition.

CAROL : DRIVE A CAB, LOSER.

MIKE : I wish to thank you for understanding. I am about to leave, and go out and get drunk, so please help me by applauding for what I have just been through-

CAROL : FIND THE WRITER AND LYNCH THE BASTARD!

MIKE : And for the guts it takes to get up and try new material.

CAROL : IT BLOWS.

MIKE : But, I'll be back. There are many other actresses and many other scenes. I will be back.

CAROL : BUT NOT WITH ME.

MIKE : But, never with her. Thank you. Thank you and good night. (He departs.)

GOING STEADY, BUT HAVING PERSONAL PROBLEMS.

TERR : This is unbelievable. This is too much. This is a holiday.

WALT : Terry.

TERR : And, we have guests! In the middle of a party, how can you do something like this?

WALT : You misunderstand.

TERR : I have eyes. You were on top of her.

WALT : I was not on top of her. She was underneath me!

TERR : And just how did that happen?

WALT : She slipped.

TERR : And fell over backwards on my bed and you happened to slip and fall on top of her?

WALT : I did not fall on her. She was passing out and-

TERR : And you were giving her mouth to breasts resuscitation?

WALT : Oh, come on-

TERR : But, I've got news, Walter; women, even stupid ones, with bad makeup, don't breathe through their tits!

WALT : I was listening for her pulse.

TERR : With your mouth?

WALT : No! It was just how it looked.

TERR : Where is she now?

WALT : In the bathroom, passed out or puking.

TERR : Oh, then you did kiss her!

WALT : I did not. God damn it! She fell down. I fell with her! That's it.

TERR : And I'm supposed to believe that?

WALT : Yes! You should. It's true.

TERR : NO! NO!

WALT : Stop shouting. You have guests!

TERR : Then open the door! Open the goddamned bedroom door and let every one hear.

WALT : Is that what you want?

TERR : Yes.

WALT : Is that what you want? Okay, okay, okay! Let's do it,
(He opens the door and starts to yell at the guests which should be the actual audience.)

WALT : Hey, everyone. Put down your pretzels and cheap wine.

TERR : And listen to this! Walt and I are having a fight. He just tried to screw one of my guests and since he's my boyfriend, I find that rude. What do you think?

WALT : That's a lie! I never touched her.

TERR : It's true. Everyone? This is Halloween, correct? A time for family and loved ones. Am I right? And Walter just went ducking for apples in the totally wrong barrel.

WALT : That's a gross exaggeration. Did you see her? Dracula, did you see her? Marie Antionette? He saw her. And, was she drunk? She was. He saw her, and he confirms that she was drunk. Okay?

TERR : Oh, what the hell does Dracula know? So, she's drunk. That makes you even more of a slob. She probably wanted no part of you.

WALT : Exactly my point! It was totally innocent.

TERR : Who is she, anyway?

WALT : I met her at the office.

TERR : YOU-YOU BROUGHT HER HERE?

WALT : Well, I had to. (To the audience.) And, if you met somebody at another party, wouldn't you invite them, if they asked you if they could come? See! It's the only polite thing to do. And, I'm being blamed because I have good manners. Is that fair?

TERR : Oh, I didn't know that you brought her here; to my party? So, while I'm walking around as the eastern half of NATO, waiting for you to arrive and complete my costume, flouncing around I am, with half of Europe hanging off my butt, you finally waltz in with Martha Washington.

WALT : Marie Antionette.

TERR : The bimbo puke machine. (To the audience.)
Is this grounds for a break-up, or not? I want to take a vote. Do I kill him or not?

WALT : Which reminds me. Will someone please go in there and see how she is? Thank you. Ladies and gentlemen, Rambos and Gizmos, all that happened was she went into the bedroom to get her cloak and she fell over and I fell on top of her. Is that so unusual? As soon as she recovers, we can ask her. She'll tell you.

TERR : Marie Antionette? A known liar. Martha Washington, yes. But, not that French slut.

WALT : Okay, let's do it. This is a democracy. Let the monsters vote.

TERR : Okay. All those in favor of this disgrace ending a four year turbulent relationship, raise your right hand.
(She counts votes.) I win! You lose.

WALT : What are you talking about? You're counting a spider as four votes!

TERR : It's my house. I can count what I want. Are you leaving?

WALT : No. Because I won.

TERR : Then I am. Good night, everyone. And Happy Halloween.

WALT : Where are you going? You're the hostess.

TERR : Quiet, traitor. Who wants to go with me?
(Grabbing people from the audience.)
Rambo? Fuzzman? Little Orphan Annie? Frankenstein and G.I. Joe! Dolly, the Sheep Clone? All seekers of truth and justice. Thank you. Let's hit the trail.
(As they depart.)

WALT : That's okay! You'll be back. You'll be back. You have to. You live here...Everybody else...Is this Halloween or not? LET'S DANCE! AND TO HELL WITH MISERY!

A FATHER ENRICHING HIS DAUGHTERS LIFE.

DAD   : Why not?

MARIE   : Because, I don't want to.

DAD   : But, Marie, you don't even know him.

MARIE   : And, that's why!

DAD   : Don't be childish. He's a man. You're a young woman.

MARIE   : And you're an old man who is always in my business.

DAD   : I'm your father. And, I think I have every right-

MARIE   : No, you don't.

DAD   : May I complete my thought? Every right to care about you and your future happiness. See the man. That's all I ask.

MARIE   : Father, this is not the sixteenth century. This is 1781. Times have changed. I'm 19 and old enough to choose the men I find interesting. I don't need help from you.

DAD   : The men you find interesting are not men. And they are not interesting.

MARIE   : How do you know? And, he's so much older than I.

DAD   : Of course, he is. Most men are. And, he's royalty.

MARIE   : I don't care.

DAD   : Marie, do you think I would recommend just anyone? He'll be here any minute.

MARIE   : Then you see him.

DAD   : Why are you so stubborn? You can't embarrass me, like this.

MARIE   : Oh,...all right. What's his name, again?

DAD   : The Marquis DeSade. How bad can he be?

MARIE   : The Marquis DeSade? Sounds stupid. I mean, Marquises are all over the place. You can hardly move without stepping over one. And what else do you know about him?

DAD   : What else is there to know? He's wealthy and available. And he is supposed to be a fun guy. And he wants to meet you. What can happen? What's he going to do? Bite you?

MARIE   : Well...I just hope he likes to dance.

DAD : The door. I'll take you to him. Remember, home by eleven. I'll be waiting up. Have fun.
(They exit. Dad comes back, pacing...looks at wall clock or watch.) Hmm, 11:15...I pray I was right. She'll never- The door! She's back. (Marie enters.)

DAD : Marie? Well?...Well? How did it go? Marie? Marie?

MARIE : Uh, like no other date I've ever had.

DAD : Was it torture? Well?...

MARIE : Father?

DAD : I mean, did you have a good time? Oh, do I see a little smile? Do I detect a tiny blush? Good! Sit down.

MARIE : No. I think I prefer to stand.

DAD : Tell Daddy, was the evening better than you expected?

MARIE : Well...it was different.

DAD : That's what a father is for! Trust experience. Now, what did you two do? How did he strike you?

MARIE : Well...in so many different ways.

DAD : Excellent! You hit it off? I knew it! Leave it to Dad. Well, tell me what you did.

MARIE : Mmmm. Mmmmmmm. Well, you know. First date. It was a bit awkward.

DAD : Where did you go?

MARIE : First to supper. Then to his Chateau.

DAD : And he offered you a fine wine. And you spoke, and in no time, the Marquis De Sade was hanging on your every word! Am I right? Am I right?

MARIE : Well, it was fairly mutual. But, Papa, how did you know?

DAD : Because, I'm no dope. You think because I'm older: "What can he know?" But, I have an inner sense. A Marquis. He did behave in a gentlemanly manner? If not-

MARIE : If not, and I'm not saying no, what would you do?

DAD : As your father, I would pay him a call and thrash him to within an inch of his life. What do you say to that?

MARIE : ...I think that he would be impressed.

DAD : Yes, he would be! And what was said on your departure?

MARIE : He's very much looking forward ...to meeting Mother.

DAD : That's what I wanted to hear. She'd be delighted. You see? You see? Can your father pick them or not? Marie, I'm proud of you. So very proud.

MARIE : Thank you, Papa. I'm worn out. Good night, Papa.
(She exits.)

DAD : Good night, Marie. Sweet dreams...YES! Now, he wants to meet my wife. This is better than I expected. So much better.
(He exits happily.)

YOU NEVER KNOW WHOM YOU'RE GOING TO MEET.

YVET : (I was in the office building lobby, looking at the wall directory. I had an audition at DD and C, for a voice over and this man walked past me, toward the elevators and I knew who he was. Just out of the corner of my eye, I had seen enough. I was 1 to 14. He was 32 to 46, but I followed him. Why? Because even with dark glasses and a soft cloth hat pulled down over his forehead, I knew...So, I stood next to him waiting for his elevator to reach the lobby. looked over; he's not that tall and I asked, my voice trembling, and I knew I was blushing, but I didn't give a damn.)
Pardon me?...But...

PAUL : Yes, it's true... I am Paul Newman.

YVET : (Paul Newman. He turned his famous face away. I thought would drop. My heart was double clutching. And then he spoke again.)

PAUL : Yes... I am Paul Newman.

YVET : (Don't arrive elevator. BREAK DOWN! I had to say something, I had to speak. How's your wife? How's your kids? Nice day? What could I say? What brings you here? No, no, no. But he had spoken to me. What was he thinking? What was Paul thinking of me?)

PAUL : (Oh, she is so beautiful. This girl is so exciting. But, not in any conventional way. She possesses both an inner and outer beauty. Oh, man, even though, I'm old enough to be her father, I'd really like to jump on her bones. I want her to be mine.)

YVET : (Oh, you don't believe it? He had that look. Women know that look. I began to sweat.)

PAUL : (I must get her name.)

YVET : MY NAME IS YVETTE TUCHINSKY!

PAUL : Oh? My kid had a turtle named Yvonne. It died of cancer.

YVET : (He spoke to me again. Paul spoke to me. Oh, he's hot for me. He knows quality. Paul, don't be shy. Go for it while you can. I'm here. I'm yours.)
I'm an actor, too.

PAUL : Really? Any luck?

YVET : (That proved it. Is that a come-on line or not? He wants my tongue between his toes.) Well, a few things.

(His elevator arrived. I got in with him. I didn't know where I was going. He pushed a floor. I pushed one higher. The door was still open.)

Mr. Newman, I've admired all your work.

PAUL : Thanks.

YVET : And, I also eat your popcorn.

PAUL : Thanks. Do you like my popcorn?

YVET : Who wouldn't?

(Oh, the way he spoke. He was so articulate. The door closed. Damn it. We started to move. I was running out of time. Paul, I really look better than this. I have a great actresses body. Taut, yet supple. Would you like to hear a monologue? It's been great getting to know you. The elevator was slowing down. No! I don't want anyone else getting on and ruining this. I... Jesus Christ. MICK JAGGER! This was some terrific building!

PAUL : MICK JAGGER!

YVET : (It was me and Paul and Mick Jagger. Mick Jagger looked over at Paul.)

PAUL : Yes, I am Paul Newman. Yes, I am Paul.

YVET : (Mick said: Sorry. Thought you were someone else. Mick didn't care! The door slid shut. Silence. Two floors more. The door opened. Mick was getting off. What was I to do? hesitated. I FOLLOWED MICK! So long, Paul. Please understand. Too late! The door closed on me. I was stuck. Ohhh, no. You try to look alluring while an elevator door pins you to a wall. I screamed: OH, CRAP! Mick never turned around. The door opened. I staggered back aboard.)

PAUL : Weren't you going to 44?

YVET : (Paul was hurt! I liked Mick Jagger more than him. I felt bad, but he'll get over it. Men love rejection. It keeps them sharp. The elevator moved to 43. His floor. He got off. I manned the threshold, once again fighting the goddamned closing door.)

Oh, Mr. Newman, it was nice meeting you. I'd love to get together and talk about the business. Can I give you my phone number?

PAUL : Why don't you ask Mick for his? Oh, and try my salad dressings. They're really good on my popcorn.

YVET : (The door closed and I rode up to 44 and got off. I had no reason to, but I did. And, I stood there, not belonging anywhere. Then I rode back down to the lobby and up to 12. I gave a great audition, but I didn't get the job. But, believe me, I didn't care. Naturally, I hurried down to the lobby and spent two hours there until the guard asked me to leave and I haven't seen either one of my boys again. But, it was a wonderful day that lifted my spirits and made me feel great to be part of the world of show business and to be living in New York.)

TRUTH AND A BURGER; BOTH HARD TO SWALLOW.

BERT : Tina, put down the burger. If you want to say something, say it. Or should I order dessert, before they run out of that, too? Ten weeks of summer stock and one coffee shop that's open till ten in a town that closes at nine. I've got to get back to New York. I must have soot. I'm going crazy.

TINA : Bert?

BERT : What?

TINA : ...It's your performance.

BERT : ...Yes? My performance? What about it?

TINA : Well...are you going to be defensive?

BERT : Could be. Let's find out. My performance?

TINA : No. You're defensive.

BERT : Tina...

TINA : Okay...your performance is not acting. It's shouting.

BERT : Of course, I'm shouting. I'm supposed to. I'm Stanley Kowalski; a life force. Should I whisper "Oh, Stella"? (He whispers.) "Oh, Stella. It's Stanley." Please.

TINA : Oh, come on, Bert. All you do is shout, shout, shout!

BERT : I do not. I find truth.

TINA : Well, find silence. You shout when you kiss me!

BERT : Tina, that's passion.

TINA : That's hell. Kissing you is like necking with a bull.

BERT : Oh, that's kind.

TINA : In Act 2, you don't enter, you invade.

BERT : I make an entrance in command of my character.

TINA : Really? Bulletin! There are other people in the play.

BERT : Oh, hey! I'm well aware of my fellow actors, whom I respect and admire as they do me as total professionals.

TINA : Then why not look at us? You're on a stage, for God's sakes, not Echo Mountain. You bellow.

BERT : Hey, the audience is totally involved with my work.

TINA : Of course. Who else can they hear?

BERT : Okay, fine, but if I'm overacting, let the director tell me. He's thrilled with my performance. One of the finest interpretations of a William's character that he's ever seen. Quote, unquote.

TINA : Oh, Bert, Bert. Don't you know?

BERT : Know what? Come on, Tina, know what? What?

TINA : About Dirk?

BERT : What about Dirk?

TINA : You don't? Are you blind as well as loud?

BERT : What the hell are you talking about?

TINA : Dirk is in love with you.

BERT : I beg your pardon? He is not.

TINA : THE DIRECTOR IS IN LOVE WITH YOU AND HE'S GAY!

BERT : Shhh! Geez, not so loud. This is South Carolina.

TINA : Dirk is in love with you and everybody knows it. Dirk Monroe is hot for your skinny male body.

BERT : Oh, God.

TINA : And, that is why he has been so very cutting to poor Polly, because he knows you can't keep your hands off her, and come on, Bert, the things you do with everybody watching... Really. Grow up. She's a kid.

BERT : That's not true. I'm not into her. We're friends.

TINA : Bert, how old is she?

BERT : Who cares? 19.

TINA : Haha ha ha haha.

BERT : 18?

TINA : 16.

BERT : No! 18. She's 18. I swear.

TINA : She's 16, 16, 16.

BERT : Quiet. She's 18. I saw her driver's license.

TINA : Learners permit. She's jailbait, you idiot.

BERT : SHHHH.

TINA : And, she's a local and have you met her mother?

BERT : No.

TINA : I have! She's a state trooper! Do you want to get us all arrested?

BERT : Waitress! Oh, Kim? Check, please? We're in a hurry.

TINA : 16, Bert. Proud? Your summer stock achievement?

BERT : Tina, maybe you're just jealous. Professionally and personally. Okay? Jealous and it shows.

TINA : Of what? I have Mark.

BERT : You've got who? Mark? You? Jack has Mark!

TINA : Jack? Jack has Mark? That's a lie.

BERT : And so has Rene, Jane and probably Dirk!

TINA : You LIAR! It's over between Jack and Mark.

BERT : No. It's over between Jack and Claire.

TINA : Jack and Claire? I thought it was Bob and Claire.

BERT : It was Bob and Claire and then Bob and Amber when it was Claire and Rick, because Tad left for a week, and before it was even you and Phil while it was me and Amber which I still regret.

TINA : Jack and Claire is over? I never knew it began.

BERT : It ended during "Oklahoma". It started during "Cats".

TINA : Everything started during "Cats". I blame the costumes.

BERT : Including me and Sara before it was Sara and Judy.

TINA : And me and Jack, before Claire dumped Phil. Mark? I am so hurt. This is what I get for loyalty.

BERT : One show is hardly loyalty. Grow up.

TINA : Under these conditions, it is. Don't look. Guess who just came in. Duck.

BERT : Dirk? Mark? Jack? Amber?

TINA : No. Mrs. Ferguson. Polly's mother.

BERT : Oh, God. In uniform?

TINA : Holster and all. It's okay. She's sitting down.

BERT : We're leaving. Leave a tip. (On their way out.)

TINA : Oh, hi, Mrs. Ferguson. Polly's such a great kid. Have you met Bert? He loves Polly, too.

BERT : Nice to meet you. We're in a hurry.

TINA : Next week, Brigadoon. It's a musical.

BERT : It's our last show. Try and see it. Next week. Brigadoon. It's a musical.

TINA : About one summer when two Americans wind up in a small town and fall in love with all the pretty, young girls.

BERT : It's a fantasy. Good night, Mrs. Ferguson. Really nice meeting you. It's been a great summer. We truly have to go.

A PROBLEM BETWEEN THE PARTNERS.
(Adapted From Claptrap.)

SARA : It's over. It's finished. That was the final straw.

FRANK : But, honey,

SARA : Don't honey me. You are a moron!

FRANK : Well, I never claimed not to be.

SARA : Don't disarm, Frank. Because if you do, I'll be the one disarming! And next to you the Venus De Milo will have arms like Popeye.

FRANK : Now, dear.......

SARA : Our anniversary! Which means half mine. And my sweet mother visits, for the first time in two years, actually sets her foot into this apartment. Here with reconciliation in her heart, tears on her powdered cheeks and what else, Mr. Moron? A check in her hand. And how much was that check for? Two thousand smackers.

FRANK : That seems to be about right.

SARA : And what did you do? Everything, but take it!

FRANK : Because, I am a man. I have a man's pride.

SARA : No. Because, you are a moron! You sat in that chair, like a limp dick.

FRANK : Sara.

SARA : I heard that on a bus. And although, I am uncertain of it's exact meaning, I have a feeling that the phrase could readily be applied to you.

FRANK : But when I refused, she smiled. She looked at me with new found respect in those beady, cold eyes.

SARA : Not respect. Relief, you asshole. Why not? She'd just saved two grand.

FRANK : And I saved my self-respect which is worth more to me than money.

SARA : No, it isn't. For five years I have suffered with you, waiting for you to complete the great American Novel, while living in the great American hovel. Complete a book? By God, you can't complete a thought!

FRANK : I can, too.

SARA   : I bring you lettuce,
FRANK   : For which I am grateful.
SARA   : And tomatoes, which I tote like a coolie. I bring you fish, because fish is brain food. Ha! You'd have to eat Moby Dick every day for a decade, just to be slow.
FRANK   : Go on, Sara, let me have it.
SARA   : Now, why have I not spoken to you since mother left, one hour and twenty minutes ago?
FRANK   : Because you're upset, which I can understand.
SARA   : Because I was giving her time to reach home. (Checks her watch.) Bingo! Now, do you know what you are going to do?
FRANK   : What?
SARA   : You are going to call her on the phone and say the following: Hi, Mom.
FRANK   : Hi, Mom.
SARA   : This is Frank. You know, Sara's husband?
FRANK   : Hi, Mom. This is Frank. You know, Sara's husband?
SARA   : Is Sara there?
FRANK   : Is Sara there?
SARA   : No? I thought she might be, because...because she was so distraught when I rejected your generous gift that she stormed out, saying that she would never come back to me unless I called you to apologize and accept your financial torrent. So, when she gets there, you can save time by just handing her the check. That should work. Sounds good. Be sincere. Got it? Sincere.
FRANK   : Got it.
SARA   : Dial.
          (He dials.)
FRANK   : It's ringing. Hi, Mom? This is Frank. Sara's Frank. Is Sara there? She left me because I didn't accept your - What? ...She is there?...Really?....
          (To Sara.) You're there and you don't want to speak to me.
SARA   : I am? Damn it, the old fox is hanging on to that dough with everything she's got. (Takes the phone.)
          Mrs. Littlefield? This is Frank's mother, Edna. May I speak

to your daughter? Thank you. (I'm coming to the phone.)
Sara? This is Edna. I know he's difficult. Hold on and talk
to Frank. You'll hang up? Then talk to......

FRANK : Sara, this is Lou. Frank's brother. Thanks, I had a great
flight. Listen...no, my mother is not butting in. Hey! Don't
you talk that way about my mom! Yours stinks! Yours is a
hyena! Haaa! Haaa! Oh, yeah?

SARA : Lou, give me the phone.
(He does.)
Hey, is this Sara? This is Lou and Frank's mother - I'm a
what? And, so is he? Hey, don't you talk about Lou like
that! You can - I never approved the marriage! You're not
good enough for my Frank. You slut! Stay with your
mother! You deserve each other.

FRANK : (Grabs the phone.)
Sara, don't listen to her. My mother doesn't mean - Who is
this? ...Mrs. Littlefield, let's compromise. Keep Sara and
give me eight hundred. Your daughter said what about me?
Okay, well, how about Lou? Maybe, she can come back to
him for five hundred. I -

SARA : (Sharing the phone.)
Littlefield, you old bag, this is Edna. Sara is an idiot. And,
so are you. You can keep your money and your daughter!
I'VE HAD ENOUGH OF BOTH OF YOU!

FRANK : And, I don't want her back! I'll live here -

SARA : With me, his mother! Goodbye, Sarah and good riddance.
(She hangs up.)

FRANK : Well...

SARA : Well, I guess that didn't work out quite as planned.

FRANK : I guess not. What's for dinner?

SARA : Sardines.

FRANK : Sardines? Well, I'm not that hungry. Let's go out.
(They exit.)

TWO FLIES IN THE OINTMENT.

FRAN : What's wrong? You ask me what's wrong?

JERR : Yeah, what's wrong?

FRAN : You call, I rush over here, it's July Fourth weekend, of all times, because you have this great idea for a play and then you come up with this!

JERR : What's wrong with this? It IS a great idea!

FRAN : Oh, come on. It's terrible.

JERR : I resent that! It happens to be fairly damned good.

FRAN : Are you crazy? Never, since Adam and Eve did dinner theater, was two flies on a corn cob, ever a good idea for a play. Jerry, it's not even a premise.

JERR : Oh, I beg to differ. It is very much a premise.

FRAN : Two flies on a corncob doesn't open up many vistas for me.

JERR : Damn it! Franny, lighten up. Two flies on a corncob is anything that our joint talents and imagination can make of it. You're just scared.

FRAN : Yes. Of you! For lack of a better word, your idea is crap.

JERR : Crap? Is that all that's bothering you? Of course, it's crap. Because, that's exactly what I want it to be.

FRAN : Oh? You intentionally want to write a play that's crap?

JERR : This time..Yes!

FRAN : Then with your experience, you won't need my help.

JERR : Maybe, I don't. Okay?

FRAN : And, may I ask just this question? Just this one question? Who on earth will want to produce a play that's crap?

JERR : A regional theater. That happens to be why they exist.

FRAN : To produce crap?

JERR : Of course! They love meaningless plays! It's the crawling actor who gets the grants. Grow up! Learn the business. That's why today the avant garde is ordinary!

FRAN : No. I have to believe in what I do.

JERR : Frannie, there's a little fly in everyone. Reach in. Dig. Find your inner insect.

FRAN : NO! Two flies are not a play.

JERR : Afraid to take the leap? An idea is like a first date. Who knows? Let's just try writing one scene. One scene. One tiny little scene.

FRAN : You really want to write about flies? Okay! Let's put it to the test.

JERR : Good girl. Computer on!

FRAN : No. You and I on. Fold your arms, big shot. Why should only actors make fools of themselves? We go first.

JERR : You think I can't? You think I can't? I can be a fly.

FRAN : Regional theaters have money. So, fly now, pay later! Two idiots on a corncob! Act one. Scene one. Fire away.

JERR : Wait. Let me set the scene. It's dusk.

FRAN : Again? In your plays it's always dusk. Why? Is it because you can't spell twi-light?

JERR : What's wrong with dusk?

FRAN : You'd be better off with total darkness.

JERR : Shh. The backyard of a July Fourth picnic.

FRAN : Rub it in.

JERR : A beautiful female fly is resting alluringly on a corn cob...

FRAN : Is that me or you?

JERR : A male fly flies in. He's tough, but kind-hearted. A bit sad, a loner, and alone on a national holiday.
(They flop their arms and buzz around.)
Hey, cousin? What's buzzin?

FRAN : I am, jerkwater. Are you deaf as well as dumb?

JERR : Say, nice looking trash.

FRAN : I beg your pardon?

JERR : Referring to the eats. Say, miss, mind if I join you?

FRAN : It's a free trashcan. Just don't step on my corns.

JERR : Good one. Boy, I love the Fourth. Don't you?

FRAN : I did. Say, flyweight, are you hitting on me?

JERR : No.

FRAN : Because, whether you know it or not, I'm happily married.

JERR : You are?

FRAN : Wait! God damn it. Not anymore. I'm now a widow!

JERR : Oh, I'm sorry.

FRAN : That's the fifth goddamned husband I've lost this summer.

JERR : Well, you still have August. How'd he go? Swatter?

FRAN : Iced coffee! Went in like a rock! I told him to stop drinking. But, no...Oh, Raoul! Raoul! I'll miss you.

JERR : I'm terribly sorry. Any children?

FRAN : 16,000...But, we were still hoping for a boy.

JERR : You have my deepest sympathies. I know what it's like to lose a loved one.

FRAN : With your face, you must. Okay, I'm over it.

JERR : Say, don't you just love these kernels?

FRAN : Say that again?

JERR : Don't you just love these kernels?

FRAN : Well, they'll do until an admiral comes along!
(They laugh uproariously.)

JERR : Man, great pairs of legs and a sense of humor. How'd you get here?

FRAN : Greyhound.

JERR : Bus?

FRAN : No.

JERR : Say, I don't mean to be rude-

FRAN : But, some things can't be helped.

JERR : But, I don't even know your name.

FRAN : Aldonza..

JERR : Oh, Spanish fly? Well, I love the tropics. Say, are you still in mourning?

FRAN : No. For the past half hour I've been in evening! (Big laugh.)

JERR : Say, would you like to dance?

FRAN : With you?

JERR : No. With Jiminy Cricket! Of course, me.

FRAN : Well, what the heck. You're a fly. I'm a fly. Life is short. In another sec, I could be a speck! LET'S ROCK!
(They dance wildly.)

JERR : Hey, baby, shake that thing.

FRAN : Whew. Thanks, sailor. I'm going to knock off and fly out for a drink of water....Don't look so sad. I'll be back.
(She flies away and returns.)

JERR : Did it work? Not bad! Well? Did it work?

FRAN : Okay. It almost worked. Not bad.

JERR : And I've got the name. "Fly By Night." Do you love it?

FRAN : Trite. So, okay, where do we go from here?

JERR : We go where all writers go. As far away from the computer as possible! I'm too excited to begin. Let's take a break.

FRAN : Good idea. Coffee. Iced coffee? (As they leave.) Hey! Can we add a hornet? Now, that would make it interesting.

JERR : No. No hornets!

FRAN : No hornets? It has to have hornets.

JERR : No hornets. This is a character study.

LOVE IN BLOOM.

MAX : Jane, I have something to tell you. I want you to know that after knowing you for five years, I really hate you.

JANE : I hope so. If you didn't, I'd be deeply disappointed. And, let me say this-

MAX : I know, the feeling-

JANE : Max, don't interrupt.

MAX : I must. Interrupting you is one of my joys.

JANE : The feeling is mutual. I loathe you.

MAX : Loathe. Nice word.

JANE : Yes. Loathing is contempt that has passed the test of time; but even loathing cannot approximate the totality of my contempt for you. The seven seas are barely a damp spot in comparison to my utter, deep, heartfelt and justified despisification of you.

MAX : Perfect. Jane, I hate you so much; will you marry me?

JANE : I beg your pardon? What are you talking about?

MAX : Jane, I don't want to lose you. How many people do we know that dislike other people and then feel guilty about it?

JANE : Oh, I run into that everywhere.

MAX : But, with us, it's the real thing.

JANE : True. When we talk about each other -

MAX : It's not petty jealousy or childish envy.

JANE : Never. It's sincere and honest appraisal. It's fact.

MAX : So, hear me out. Now, this may sound cynical-

JANE : So far, not overly.

MAX : If we marry, then we are more or less guaranteed a lifetime of being able to despise each other on a very intense round-the-clock basis. I'll have something to live for.

JANE : I like that. I do. That could work.

MAX : And, then, I could be almost certain of ruining your life.

JANE : At the very least, we'd both have the chance.

MAX : We can start where most other couples end up!

JANE : And even better, unlike them, there'll be no shattered dreams,

MAX : No lost hopes. No disillusionment.

JANE : By God! You may have come up with the solution for the terribly high divorce rate. Marry someone you already hate! And you'll never be disappointed. This is brilliant!

MAX : We'll never divorce. Why would we? The reason we're marrying is NOT to get along.

JANE : And we could begin immediately. During the wedding.

MAX : The minister says: You may kiss the bride. And I'll say: Are you crazy? You kiss her.

JANE : And, I'll let him! Kiss me, Minister! Anything is better than this pig.

MAX : That's the spirit. Cheap and vulgar. Never lose it.

JANE : Max, we could cheat on each other and never feel guilty.

MAX : And, unlike other married men, I'd never worry if I was losing your love.

JANE : Because you never had it.

MAX : No marriage counseling, doubts, or romantic anorexia.

JANE : If only more married people just accepted the fact that they don't like each other, have little in common save for the need to be liked-

MAX : In most cases; there are exceptions- what's mutual is an ever growing boredom and disgust.

JANE : And used that as a starting point...things could only get better, not worse!

MAX : So,...for those reasons; Jane, will you marry me?

JANE : Of course! Absolutely! But, then, what if we-

MAX : After living together for a while-

JANE : Actually, begin liking, well you begin liking me.

MAX : Not possible- but, you might- I am handsome. Then, whom would we have to despise?

JANE : Oh, no. We would stand to lose everything.

MAX : Darn it. But, if our resolve weakens...Jane? IN-LAWS! YES!

JANE : MAX! IN-LAWS! A constant reminder of what it is that we don't like about each other! Whew. I am so excited. This could be the start of something dreadful! I can't wait to tell my friends. We're getting married!
(They start to laugh.)

94

MAX : We're getting married.

JANE : Let's do it on Halloween.

MAX : In costumes! I can be Death.
(They are laughing hysterically.)

JANE : I can be Taxes! By gosh, this could be fun.
(They skip around, arm in arm and skip off.)
We're getting married. We're getting married. And, this ones-

MAX : For kreeps!

JANE : For kreeps!

DECISIONS, DECISIONS.
Two actors anywhere.

KAREN : It's a great opportunity; grab it.

BERT : But, Karen, I don't know if it's the right one.

KAREN : Bert, for God's sakes, your first role in New York after three years. Grab it and make it work.

BERT : Right. You're right. Thank you.

KAREN : I mean, are you nude? Do you eat body parts? What?

BERT : Well, first of all, it's a play about the Korean war.

KAREN : The what war?

BERT : Korean.

KAREN : Drama or comedy?

BERT : Drama.

KAREN : The Korean War? Is it fictional?

BERT : No, there actually was one.

KAREN : Really? I never heard of it.

BERT : See?

KAREN : That doesn't mean anything. It could be one of those quiet wars with a large cult following. Who was in it?

BERT : Us and Korea. China and maybe Ireland. I couldn't tell.

KAREN : Okay. Reputable countries. So, what is your problem?

BERT : Well, who's going to come and see it?

KAREN : No one. It's a showcase. Have you read the script?

BERT : Twice.

KAREN : Good?

BERT : I have no idea. I asked the director what it meant.

KAREN : Before you read it, or after you read it?

BERT : Before. I didn't want to read it and still not know.

KAREN : Smart. Very professional. And he said?

BERT : He's not quite sure, but he thinks it's a metaphor.

KAREN : I like that. I respect any director that can turn what he doesn't understand into a metaphor. I think a heartfelt vagueness is essential to the success of any play.
Are you a soldier?

BERT : Yes. I open the show.

KAREN : Fantastic.

BERT : With three lines.

KAREN : To open the show? Good. Very good.

BERT : No, I have three lines for the entire show. The curtain rises. I'm in a foxhole. I stand and shout: "Look! An eagle! A free bird in flight. How I envy your proud plumage!" That's it.

KAREN : That's a very nice speech.

BERT : And BANG! I get it. A sniper. Offstage. And after that I lie there. Dead. That's it. I'm dead.

KAREN : For how long do you lie there or is it lay?

BERT : Either way, two hours. No intermission. Two hours of my back to the audience. The director doesn't want them to see my face, because my nose could twitch. So I ask, Karen,... do you think that this is the New York debut that will advance my career?

KAREN : Bert, are you crazy? A lot of actors would kill for that role. Do the lines. I want to hear. Do them. Do them. Please.
(He reveals a huge script.)

BERT : Performance level? From beginning to end?

KAREN : Yes. Let's find out what they mean.
(He prepares.)

BERT : Okay....I'm not really sure, yet. But, here goes...
(He lies down, gets up.)
Wait! Help me. Be the eagle. Fly. Fly like an eagle.

KAREN : Good idea. Focus on me. I'm on my perch. Here I go! I'm flying. Do eagles make sounds?

BERT : If they want to, sure.
(She flies around.)

KAREN : Cooo...Cooo. Watch the birdie.

BERT : No, no. You're flying like a parakeet. Be grand. Big wings. Swoop. Soar. Better. Much better. Yes!

KAREN : Ready? Here, I come. The form, the face of a hunter.
(She is flying. He jumps to his feet.)

BERT : Look! An eagle! A free bird in flight. How I envy your proud plumage!

KAREN : Gunshot!

BERT : Bang. Aggghhh....aghhhhhhh...

(He twists and as he is falling:)

KAREN : Ohhhhh. (She too is falling.)

BERT : MA! I'M DYING! I love you, ...Maaa. Ohhhhh.
(He hits the floor, she lands on top of him. They get up.)
Well?

KAREN : Wow! You must do the part! You were so real.

BERT : Thank you. Did you like the ad-lib? About my mother? I had to do it. But, what the hell were you doing? It was my scene and you landed on me.

KAREN : He shot me, too. I couldn't help it. I was so into it. But, you were communicating so much of .....you know, death, pain, grief. All that stuff.

BERT : I feel it. God damn it! I wasn't sure, but now I know. I'm an actor. And I must act!

KAREN : No question about it. You can do this. It may be three lines, but on your resume, it'll look like a lead.

BERT : Thank you, Karen. I needed to hear that. Now, this brings me to my next question.

KAREN : What? What else is there?

BERT : Should I invite agents?

KAREN : Absolutely. They leave at intermission anyway. Bert, you haven't mentioned my eagle.

BERT : Very good. Very helpful. You had a real sense of bird.

KAREN : Thank you. And call your parents and let them know.

BERT : I'll have to write. They just got an unlisted number. Then it's settled. I'm going to do it. My first play in New York. It may not be much, but after my lines, I'll get plenty of much needed rest. I just hope I don't fall asleep.

KAREN : And, you don't know. In this business, you never know.

BERT : It could lead to something. Come on, let's get out of here and go rent a movie. Look, look an eagle in flight. I'll take the script. I may want to make some changes.
(They exit.)

MARRIED COUPLE WATCHING TV.

WOM : Honey, are you listening to me?

MAN : Huh? What?

WOM : I said, are you listening to me?

MAN : Of course, dear...Do I have a choice?

WOM : Excuse me? What does that mean?

MAN : What does what...Oh, it doesn't mean anything.

WOM : No, dear, I think it does. Which is remarkable, being that most things you do say rarely do mean anything. But, in this case, I think you actually have expressed what one might call, a feeling.

MAN : Really? Why, thank you.

WOM : Yes! I think you may think that I talk too much. Do you?

MAN : Well...honey, I think you have just answered yourself.

WOM : Well, sweetheart, the reason I may talk too much is that I must tell you what to do, because unless I do tell you what to do, and repeat it ten times, you don't do anything or pay any attention to me, at all!

MAN : Margaret, please? I'm trying to watch television.

WOM : Oh, you can pay attention to television, to that drivel, but not to me!

MAN : Okay! I'll turn off the T.V. and listen to your drivel. Go ahead. You're free to driv. I've turned off the TV. I've turned off my enjoyment. In fact, I've even turned off the highway to happiness, because of you, my wife, who happens to be, the biggest turn off of them all!

WOM : Oh, really? Oh, really, Senor Sunshine? That's it! I've been insulted by you for the last and final time.

MAN : Don't bet on it.

WOM : I do. Because I am leaving!

MAN : You're leaving? Now? Don't tease me.

WOM : So long, sap.

MAN : Oh, no. You're not leaving me.

WOM : And tell me why I shouldn't, wouldn't or couldn't.

MAN : Because, I'm leaving you. I am the leaver! You are the leaveree. I leave! You loaf! I live! So long. It's over.

WOM : You fool! This simply shows just how stupid you are. The woman always leaves the fat, dull man. So, sit down.

MAN : Oh, no. I'm leaving you! Okay, let's leave together.

WOM : Impossible. If we both leave, then whom are we leaving? There'll be no one left to be left. And when we've left, who's going to be left to watch what's left after we're gone?

MAN : Right. So, in that case, let's not leave anything to be left, okay? In other words, let's take it all, now! Chair!

WOM : Take it. Take the couch. Take the rugs. I don't care.

MAN : Oh, no you don't. You're not sticking me with the couch. I hate this couch. It's as lumpy as you are!

WOM : Fine. I've taken lumps for years. I'll take a few more, because I've taken everything from you that anyone can take.

MAN : Oh, is that so? Well, then, please take something you like.

WOM : It won't be you.

MAN : I refer to your best friend, the huge refrigerator.

WOM : I don't want the goddamned refrigerator.

MAN : You should. It's your favorite part of the house!

WOM : Why not? It's smarter than you are and it weighs less!

MAN : Oh, look at you! There are two man made structures visible from outer space. The Great Wall of China and your ass.

WOM : And you'll never see either. Take the refrigerator. Take the TV. Take the Learning Channel. You're so dumb, you think The Great Castles of Europe is a movie! You keep waiting for Ivanhoe.

MAN : And you watch Sally Jesse and wait for wisdom. Here! Take books! I hate books.

(They are throwing things at each other.)

WOM : Take magazines. And papers. Take the subscriptions. Take the opinions. And the desk!

MAN : Take the lamps. Take lights. Take the electricity out of the walls!

WOM : Take the pictures. Take the walls!

MAN : You want me to take the walls? OKAY! YOU TAKE THE WALLPAPER! I'LL TAKE THE WALLS!

(He is trying to rip down the walls.)

WOM : AND THE CEILING. YOU'VE HIT IT. SO, TAKE IT.

MAN : THEN TAKE THE FLOORS! Take the air!

WOM : Take a bath.

MAN : Take a walk. Take the roof.

WOM : Take my hair.

MAN : Here! Take the shirt off my back! (He rips his shirt off.) And take the back that's under my shirt.

WOM : Take shoes! You freak. (She throws her shoes at him.) Take my teeth! Take the house! Take the universe. Take- (The doorbell rings. The room is a shambles. A long pause.)

WOM : Take-...Honey, was that the door?

MAN : Whose door?

WOM : Your door. My bell.

MAN : Oh, my goodness...

WOM : What?

MAN : Reverend Miller and his wife. They said they might drop by.

WOM : Reverend Miller? Now? Your Reverend. My wife.

MAN : Gee, how do we explain this? This is embarrassing.

WOM : Humiliating I- I've got it! The Rummage sale! Perfect.

MAN : The Rummage sale. But, Goddamn it. He'll take everything!

WOM : Then, we'll have nothing.

MAN : Less to carry. I'll get my door.

WOM : I'll start my tea.

MAN : Your cups.

WOM : Your bags. Put on my brave front, darling and-

MAN : Yes? My yes, your darling.

WOM : Answer your door.

MAN : My answer. Our mess. Reverend Miller? I'm coming!

THE MAKING OF A DEAL.

(Two writers circling a telephone. Ready to pounce.)

ELLEN : Herbie, what are you going to tell them?

HERB : I don't know. This is so unfair.

ELLEN : We never hear from them at all. But now that they're in a bind, they call. "Do you have any ideas?"

HERB : Well, we have half an idea.

ELLEN : Which they'll hate. Because it STINKS!

HERB : But, it's Mike Bush. It's the Manhattan Theater Club. It's big time. They produce Terrance McNally.

ELLEN : So what? Would they ask Terrance to write a one act play for $500? A pathetic amount that we have to split.

HERB : But, the opportunity. This could lead to something.

ELLEN : Sure. To two nervous breakdowns! They don't care what happens to us. We're nothing to them.

HERB : Well, probably not.

ELLEN : I'm just so tired of being put under pressure by total strangers; tired of existing, waiting for the phone to ring. Waiting to be wanted for most of your adult life can be devastating. "We need a short play. What do you have? Call you tomorrow at three." And we suffer.

HERB : It's ten after three.

ELLEN : And, then they make you wait! And pace and sweat and wait for what? An opportunity to fail; which is what they really want. Why? Because our failure substantiates their superiority which is what they live for. And you know I'm speaking the truth. Well?

HERB : Maybe, he won't call.

ELLEN : Oh, he will. He won't miss the chance to hear us beg. (The phone rings.) Aha! Okay, Herb. You're on. It's hello and grovel time. (He picks up the phone.)

HERB : Hello?...Mike? How you doing? Okay? What do we have? Well...Mike? Okay, I'll hold. He wants me to hold.

ELLEN : There it is! They call us, and put us on hold! Hold while I fart. Hold while I scratch. Hold while I talk to someone much more important than you are, which could be the

102

delivery boy. Hold! Hold! Hold! How can you take it?
How deeply insulting. How incredibly rude.

HERB : But, Ellen, God damn it, it is the Manhattan Theatre Club.

ELLEN : So what? We are as important as they are. Just who the
hell do they think they are?

HERB : I...Mike? What have I come up with? What have me and
my partner come up with? Okay, I'll tell you. The sudden
and crystal clear realization, Mr. Bush, that you're an idiot.
Nothing but an idiot.

ELLEN : Herb!

HERB : An idiot! Why? One, because, you're talking to me and
two: because of what you do for a living; theater! Which is
the same thing as welfare. GET A JOB!

ELLEN : Herb! Give me the phone. (They are struggling over the
receiver.) Give me the phone.

HERB : And that goes for you-

ELLEN : Herb, give me the goddamned phone!

HERB : and your fat boss, Lynne Meadows! That aging lesbian!

ELLEN : Herb! No! Give me the phone!

HERB : She's a dyke, and if she isn't, she should be. And if you
were a woman, you'd be one, too. And, now, my partner is
dying for the phone, because she hates your useless guts
more than I do. Ellen, tell him! Ellen, speak your mind.
(Hands Ellen the phone. She stares at it. He takes it
back.)

HERB : That was Ellen. Too much of a lady to express her
contempt.

ELLEN : Oh, Jesus.

HERB : Oh, you think I'm funny? Well, Bush League, let me tell you
what you are. You're a production pimp. A desk dork! THE
ONLY THING YOU CAN DO IS XEROX! What does your
mother think of you? Is she proud of what her son does for
a living? YOU FAILURE!! I may write crap, but remember,
you get paid to copy it! SO COPY THIS! BANG! (Herb
slams down the phone.) Well?...Well, now, what do you
think of me? (She stares at him. Long moments pass.
The phone rings. She pounces on it.)

ELLEN : Hello? Mike? This is Ellen Ravine. Mike, I- You loved the idea? Two insane writers turning on their producer can be hilarious. Keep it fast, but give it more pathos. He thinks it's fresh and original. It has real promise. The best idea he's heard today. Five hundred dollars. Can we get in a draft in a week?...Well, I don't see why not. We can try. Thank you, Mike. Great talking to you. Can we get half up front? You have his address? Swell. We're very excited. Good. Bye. (She hangs up.) We have it! You were brilliant!

HERB : I was? But I meant every word.

ELLEN : And, that's why it was good. It was unique. Oh, they only want ten minutes. We have an entire week.

HERB : But, I thought you-

ELLEN : Hate him? Of course. Hey, I hate my landlord too, but am I moving? Hell, no. So?

HERB : So...So, gee, let's start working.

ELLEN : Let's start. Do you want to start by writing, or do you want to start by taking a break?

HERB : Let's start by taking a break. I've got to get out of here. It's amazing. Amazing. Sincerity really sells. I wonder if there is anything else that I can be sincere about?

ELLEN : Let's not worry about that now. Coffee? And a pastry?

HERB : Something sweet. Something very sweet. (They exit together.)

ELLEN : Herb, partner, thanks to you we got a job.

NERVES OF STEEL.
An actress meets an agent.

YVET : (To the audience.)
Did I look good? I looked great. And right on time. Okay, a few minutes late for lunch. But, I was not going to seem too eager and men in suits like to wait.

LARR : Yvette? Yvette. Come with me. Our table is ready. Hungry? Food's exceptional.

YVET : He was waiting for me at the bar. Larry Steele of Steele Talent and Associates.

LARR : I can recommend the pasta and the Chicken Scarpariello is right up there...if you like chicken. Wine? White or red? Either goes. How about both? Why not?

YVET : My first real meeting with a real agent. I mean I'd had several two minute wastes of time in offices: "Photo and Resume. Let me know when you're in something, I'll try to come down. But, you have to understand.", crap.

LARR : Let's start off with salad. House? I think so.

YVET : He'd seen me in "The Velvet Pizza" Off Broadway. Okay, off off...a theatrical disgrace, but I was good, and after the performance, we only did six, a card for me and now this, and my heart was pounding. Did it show? And Verdicchio; chilled. A real meal. My first professional munch.

LARR : Well, Yvette, let me tell you, may I be honest?

YVET : Larry Steele, a little sleaze, some grease, a nice tie.

LARR : Because, if we're going to know each other, do business, I pull no punches. Straight to the jaw. That's who I am. That's what, where, and why I am. Where was I? Breadstick?

YVET : That's the way I am too, Larry.

LARR : The play you were in? Off the top? What the hell was it?

YVET : Good question. I wondered about that, myself.

LARR : Stinko. Separate and re-cycle. But, you? A word...star.

YVET : Oh, thank you. Thank you so very much.

LARR :   Next word...talent. A real force on that stage. Magic. The scene, I loved it, when you punched your mother in the face- By the way, was she really bleeding?

YVET :   It was an accident. I usually miss.

LARR :   Smacked her, not for hiding your drugs, but for using them. "Ma, one addict in the family is enough! Let it be me." You see, I remember. Powerful. Strong, but...also tender.

YVET :   I tried for that. I'm so glad that you saw my intention.

LARR :   Kid, you were fabulous. Anyway, eat. It'll get cold.

YVET :   Oh, no. Let's talk. What else?

LARR :   So, what's on the agenda? What's coming up for Yvette Tuchinsky? By the way, I love the name; it takes nerve.

YVET :   Well, actually...

LARR :   Making ends meet? Great bread. Boyfriend?

YVET :   Sort of.

LARR :   Roommates?

YVET :   Two; legal aid and circus clown. Both working.

LARR :   Because this is what I have in mind,   Yvette...Oh,   waiter... Burro? That's butter. Grazie. What was I saying?

YVET :   This is what you have in mind. Yes? What? Yes? Hmmm?

LARR :   Yvette,

YVET :   He leaned across the table and what he said next was breath- taking and totally vital.

LARR :   A future for you. Not future small F. I don't play small. I mean future whopping gigantic big huge F.

YVET :   Big F...he sees me, Yvette Tuchinsky, big, whopping F.

LARR :   This is me and my operation. Select, but hugely successful. I'm not a rancher with a herd. I'm a connoisseur with prize beef! And I see Blue Ribbons pasted all over your charming chest. Why? Because, you've got it!

YVET :   Thank you. Thank you. Thank you, Larry.

LARR :   I'm talking movies. Is that what you want? If you don't, tell me now. Movie work or no?

YVET :   Well, I...

LARR :   You're not one of these actresses whose above Hollywood and knocking down five or six million a flick?

YVET : Oh, please, no. My first love is theater, but I'd do a film if the part was right.

LARR : Good. Okay. We kick it off in New York. Some commercials, theater. Get you seen. In a year, the coast. It's ugly, but necessary. You start meeting people. Okay?

YVET : Of course. I love to meet people.

LARR : Good. Producers, directors and more important, the inside power, the fire of the furnace. I get 15%, goes to 20 for any contract over a million. Do we have a deal? Do we have a deal? Do we? Do we? Say yes. Say yes. Do we?

YVET : Yes!

LARR : WE HAVE A DEAL! Shake. And, a little kiss. DESSERT! Give me two days, and I'll call. Yvette,...are you ready? Are you ready to get the fame you deserve and can you handle it? Are you ready to be ready?

YVET : Yes, I am. I am very ready. A hug goodbye, and home on a cloud. And on the phone to everyone. Mother. Aunts. Strangers! Four years and I'm on my way. Two days, no call. Three days, no call and then I saw it. Larry Steele. Front page. New York Post. Shot dead by a hooker! His hooker. Larry Steele was no agent. LARRY STEELE WAS A GODDAMNED PIMP!

LARR : No, don't shoot! Please. I got a kid in Penn State!

YVET : Larry. My Larry. Murdered by one of his call girls. My acting career lying in a pool of cold- blooded blood. What kind of a pig was he? YOU'RE A PIG! A PIG!

LARR : Saint Peter? Hi. Larry Steele. My pleasure.

YVET : Did he really like my performance? I think he did.

LARR : Saint, may I call you Peter? Great. Listen, I've been up here, on appeal, for a few days and I've noticed, there is very little going on at night. Should that be? Now, Pete, by the way, I'm totally knocked out by the job you do,...I have a little idea... All these dead women doing nothing...

YVET : He touched me! YEGHHHHH! But, I have to admit, the chicken was superior and I've been felt up by worse for less. What actress hasn't? I'll get over it. I will. God damn it! I already have...MAAAAA.

About the Author . . .

_____

Ken Friedman was born and raised in New York City. Following four years in the Navy, he attended the University of Florida. He returned to New York and wrote material for Johnny Carson, The Bob Newhart Specials, the Dean Martin Roasts and others. His play Claptrap was presented by the Manhattan Theatre Club in 1987 and has had numerous productions in the United States and abroad.

35 For Two is his second book.